COOKED IN AFRICA

A Cooking Journey Through Southern Africa

Justin Bonello

PENGUIN BOOKS

Published by the Penguin Group
Penguin Books (South Africa) (Pty) Ltd, 24 Sturdee Avenue, Rosebank, Johannesburg 2196, South Africa
Penguin Group (USA) Inc, 375 Hudson Street, New York, New York 10014, USA
Penguin Group (Canada), 90 Eglinton Avenue East, Suite 700, Toronto, Ontario, Canada M4P 2Y3
(a division of Pearson Penguin Canada Inc)
Penguin Books Ltd, 80 Strand, London WC2R 0RL, England
Penguin Ireland, 25 St Stephen's Green, Dublin 2, Ireland (a division of Penguin Books Ltd)
Penguin Group (Australia), 250 Camberwell Road, Camberwell, Victoria 3124, Australia
(a division of Pearson Australia Group Pty Ltd)
Penguin Books India Pvt Ltd, 11 Community Centre, Panchsheel Park, New Delhi – 110 017, India
Penguin Group (NZ), 67 Apollo Drive, Mairangi Bay, Auckland 1310, New Zealand
(a division of Pearson New Zealand Ltd)

Penguin Books (South Africa) (Pty) Ltd, Registered Offices:
24 Sturdee Avenue, Rosebank, Johannesburg 2196, South Africa

www.penguinbooks.co.za

First published by Penguin Books (South Africa) (Pty) Ltd 2009
Reprinted 2010
Copyright © Cooked in Africa Films 2009

ALL RIGHTS RESERVED
THE MORAL RIGHT OF THE AUTHOR HAS BEEN ASSERTED

ISBN 978 0 143 02604 4

Written by Justin Bonello and Martin Raubenheimer
Design and layout by twoshoes.co.za
Cover design by twoshoes.co.za
Photography by Duane Howard and Evan Haussmann
Printed and bound by 1010 Printing International Ltd, China

CONTENTS

FOREWORD

This book is a compilation of places, spaces, flavours and fascinations that I focused on while filming my cooking travel series 'Cooked', and it combines my three favourite things - Southern Africa, food and friends.

My personal gastronomic journey began when my late gran taught me to make pancakes (*I still have her pan many years down the line*) and during weekends and school holidays spent in the great outdoors either on the Breede River or on the Wild Coast in the Eastern Cape. This humble start was where I can truly say I began my love affair with cooking and wide-open spaces and my fascination with all the treasures of the sea.

By the time I reached my twenties I was getting it. The more you're out there playing, the more you understand the simple truths of food and life and how everything is interconnected.

And when you add into this mix the beauty of travel, of getting out there, of searching for those elements that make you tick, of making friends and memories, life is truly grand.

Today, I am still just a simple cook – I'm like any other South African, outside next to the braai, burning his fingers, cracking a can of lager and cooking for mates – but I hope that this book will inspire you to be a little more adventurous and to extend your repertoire.

Without exception, we all have flops from time to time - but, like life, food is about experimenting, trying new things, making good friends and, most of all, having fun. It's all part of the process and when it works the rewards are sweet - or savoury!

Just remember, those of you lucky enough to find yourselves in my marvellous part of the world have a duty not only to relish all that's on the menu but also to do so in a manner that's sustainable - I'd like my children to be able to experience my kind of life as well.

For those living farther afield and far from the veld - welcome to Southern Africa: it's a Moerse Lekker Place.

Justin Bonello
Cook, Traveller and Lover of Life

cooked // *translation* ① To have an unrestrained outlook on life. ② *informal* To be so infatuated with something that one seems fanatical, loopy or insane. 'That's cooked.' ③ Off one's trolley. ④ To make food edible; Cooked to perfection.

Justin's colloquialisms & other translations

AFRICAN TV - *campfire*
BABBALAS - *hung over*
BEDONDERED - *go crazy*
BLATJANG - *chutney*
BLÊRRIE - *excessively*
BOEREKOS - *local dishes made on farms*
BOET - *brother*
BRAAI - *barbecue*
BUNDU - *wild, sparsely populated region*
CHIRP / TUNE - *friendly banter*
DERM - *intestine*
DOF - *stupid*
DOP - *booze*
DUK - *fat*
DUMPIE - *small can of beer*
EINA! EINA! EINA! - *Ouch! Ouch! Ouch!*
GAAN TE KERE - *go wild*
GESONDHEID - *cheers*
GOOI - *throw*
HOENDER - *chicken*
HOWZIT - *short for 'how is it?'*
ISIDUDU - *crusty sediment*
JOL - *party*
KAALVOET - *barefoot*
KRAAL - *pen/paddock*
KOP SEER - *pounding headache produced by a hangover*
KOS - *food*
KLAP - *smack*
KREEF - *crayfish*
KUIER - *to visit and party on down*
LEKKER - *nice*

MAAKIE SAAKIE - *all good*
MOER - *bash*
MOER KOFFIE - *ground coffee*
MOERSE DRONK - *very drunk*
MOERSE LEKKER - *very nice*
MUNG - *bash*
'N BOER MAAK 'N PLAN - *a person will find a way*
NOGAL - *as well*
NOW NOW / JUST NOW - *any length of time from shortly to in a while*
OKES - *guys*
OUMA - *grandmother*
OU TANNIES - *old aunties*
PADKOS - *food one eats while travelling*
PAP - *soft porridge*
POTJIE POT - *three-legged cast iron pot*
SCHLEP - *big hassle*
SKOP - *kick*
SLAGGED - *slaughtered*
SLAP GAT - *very lazy*
SLEG - *useless*
SPOEK AND DIESEL - *brandy and coke*
STUK - *piece*
TEN PAST THIRSTY - *time to drink*
TANNIE - *aunt*
VELD - *bush/wilderness*
VETKOEK - *sweet/savoury balls of deep fried dough*
VLEI/S - *dam or marshy area*
VLEIS - *meat*
WACK - *load, big piece*

Atlantic Ocean

WEST
COAST

● Elands Bay

6

2

5

CAPE WINELANDS

3

● Cape Town

1 4

● Hermanus

AGULHAS
NATIONAL
PARK

CAPE
POINT

WESTERN CAPE

GARDEN ROUTE

George

Knysna

● Stilbaai

Indian Ocean

N

CAPE EXPLORATIONS

W edged slap bang between the city and suburbia, Table Mountain is every Capetonian's little piece of heaven. In reality it's the heart and lungs of the Mother City but when you're on top of it, and one kilometre above the hustle and bustle of city life, it's easy to forget about all the worries of the world - which is just one of the many reasons why we Capetonians are so proud and protective of our Mountain. And what better meal to offer those who have succumbed to her charms than a hearty plate of some of her residents' signature dishes - manna from heaven.

The average South African would probably say that braaivleis was our national dish, but down in the Cape, bobotie rules the coast. Slaves who came to the Cape from Indonesia, Java and the surrounding islands brought with them the exotic spices that make this dish so special. Its presentation is similar to that of an English Shepherd's Pie or a Greek Moussaka, but it boasts a somewhat more complex layer of flavours than either of those. And, besides, it tastes moerse lekker.

BOBOTIE

★★★★ **THIS RECIPE SERVES 4** ★★★★

Preheat your oven to 180°C. Heat the butter in a pan, add the onion and allow to sweat and sweeten. Remove from the pan and set aside. Next, reheat the pan over a high heat and fry the beef and pork mince in their own fat until brown. Now remove from the heat and add the onions together with all the other ingredients except the milk and the eggs. Mix well and then spoon into an ovenproof dish, the mince should be 3 - 4cm deep. Using the back of a wooden spoon spread the mixture evenly in the bottom of your dish. Whisk the eggs and milk together and pour over the mince. Bake until the egg custard sets. A good way to make sure it's cooked is to do the wobble-test. If it still has the consistency of instant pudding whack it back in the oven for a little longer until it's cooked through and nicely golden brown. Serve hot or cold with loads of blatjang and a green salad, or be traditional and serve it hot with yellow rice.

YELLOW RICE *(to go with Bobotie)*

1 cup basmati rice

a dash of salt

a pinch of turmeric

2 sticks cinnamon

a handful of raisins
  - *soaked in water for 20 minutes, then drained*

Prepare the rice as usual, but add the turmeric and cinnamon sticks. Once the rice is cooked remove the cinnamon sticks and only then add the raisins - this prevents them from turning into the consistency of mushy-peas.

INGREDIENTS

small knob of butter

1 large onion - *chopped*

250 g minced beef

250 g minced pork

a couple of cloves of garlic
  - *crushed*

a small hand of ginger
  - *peeled and grated*

a big pinch of garam masala

½ teaspoon turmeric

a pinch of ground cumin
  and coriander

a couple of cloves

3 allspice berries

a pinch of dried mixed herbs

a handful of dried apricots
  - *chopped*

a small handful of flaked
  almonds

3 teaspoons apricot chutney

4 teaspoons chopped parsley

4 bay leaves - *plus extra to garnish*

a handful of sultanas

250ml of full cream milk

3 large free range eggs

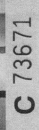

SOUTH AFRICAN NATIONAL PARKS

HOERIKWAGGO TRAIL

As you drive out of almost any big, bad South African city it won't be too long before you're drawn to one or other of the numerous farm stalls that nestle amongst the flora and fauna on the side of our national roads. There's no doubt that they transport us back to steamy kitchens, rich sweet smells and loving indulgences - oumas and tannies with big laps and even bigger hearts. I can visualise wooden shelves crammed with jars of home-made jams, relishes, pickles, sliced biltong, salty yellow butter and warm farm bread. We might have moved out, on and even up but some things still are best when they're made by hand. Maybe it's because they're not so perfect that they seem just right and that's exactly why you should have a go at making them yourself.

HOMEMADE BLATJANG
SWING BACK TO OUMA'S TABLE

Apricot Blatjang // This is an original Cape Malay recipe and even though Mrs Balls is a national treasure, it's always going to be better when you make it yourself.

Halve and stone the apricots. Place all the ingredients together in a stainless steel saucepan *(don't use brass, copper or iron - the vinegar reacts with these metals and will give your chutney a not-so-lekker metallic flavour).* Bring slowly to the boil and then simmer for 45 minutes to an hour, stirring occasionally until the chutney is the consistency of jam and has a syrupy sheen to it.

Bottle in sterilised hot jars and seal immediately.

Blatjang is the perfect accompaniment for biscuits and cheese, but it is especially good with bobotie. The basic recipe has been around for ever but tastes change with the times so, once you've mastered the concept, go ahead and experiment . . .

To Sterilise Jars *there are just two cardinal rules:*
① *Always sterilise the jars by washing them in a dishwasher, or rinse in boiling water and then heat in a medium oven or microwave for 10 minutes.* ② *Refrigerate the jars once they've been opened.*

INGREDIENTS

2 kg ripe apricots

1 large onion
 - *peeled and chopped*

2 cloves of garlic
 - *finely chopped*

250g seedless raisins

400 g brown sugar

a small pinch of cayenne pepper

pinch of salt

a small knob of ginger
 - *finely grated*

a small dollop of fresh hot English mustard

500ml cider vinegar

A

PICKLED ONIONS

to go with anything but best served with strong mature cheddar

Important: Don't use copper, brass or iron pans for this because the vinegar will react with the metal and this will give your pickled onions a metallic flavour. Rather use a stainless steel pan.

Make the brine by slowly heating the salt in the water until it's all dissolved. Allow it to cool. Next, prick the onions once and submerge them in the cooled brine for a couple of days - use a clean stone or anything heavy to make sure your onions stay submerged. Dry the onions and pack them tightly into a sterilised jar *(see page 14)*, sprinkle a couple of teaspoons of the mixed pickling spices over them, add the malt vinegar, seal and shake well. Put the jar in a cupboard and forget about it for a month or so. After that the onions will be mature enough to eat and their flavour will continue to improve over time. Remember to refrigerate the jar after opening it.

PS: Try to use a jar with a plastic inner cover – that will prevent the vinegar's acidity from reacting with the metal and affecting the taste.

INGREDIENTS

225 g sea salt *(not table salt)*

3 litres water

1 kg packet of pickling onions or small peeled white onions

pickling spice - *a combination of a pinch each of mace, cinnamon, allspice berries, black peppercorns, plus 4 cloves and 1 bird's eye chilli*

malt vinegar

Mace is the waxy red covering of the nutmeg seed. Buy the blades and grind them yourself and use in desserts and roasts. It's best if you add a little just before serving, as cooking changes the flavour and might make it a tad bitter.

This golden oldie is a goodie. It's eternally popular and never dates. As one of my all-time favourite puds, I've experimented over the years with many a variation and modification and here I share with you my tried and trusted, most successful combination – scored from an ou tannie at one of the restaurants where I worked as a waiter in my late teens. Please, when I say CUP, I mean 250 ml. Baking is an exact science - get the quantities wrong, and the only thing I can guarantee is a flop.

MALVA PUDDING
MY ULTIMATE FAVOURITE

✸✸✸✸✸ THIS RECIPE SERVES 6 TO 8 ✸✸✸✸✸

METHOD Beat the sugar and the eggs in a bowl until the mixture is fluffy and the sugar granules have disintegrated (*you can use an electric beater to make this easier*), then add the apricot jam and mix it all up. In another bowl sift the flour, bicarb and salt together at least twice. Next, melt the butter and add the vinegar and the milk. (*If the butter is too hot, the mixture will curdle and you'll have to chuck it - so don't superheat the butter/milk/vinegar mixture.*) Now add the dry mix and the butter/milk/vinegar mix alternately to the egg mix, folding in well.

Pour the mixture evenly into a butter-greased muffin tray (*one with 12 muffin cups*). Each muffin cup should be about half filled. Bake in a preheated oven at 180°C for between 45 minutes and 1 hour. Because of all the sugar, you can cook the pud until it's nice and brown.

WHAT YOU'LL NEED

1 cup sugar

2 large eggs at room temp.

1 tablespoon smooth apricot jam

1¼ cups cake flour

1 teaspoon bicarbonate of soda

a pinch of salt

2 tablespoons butter

1 teaspoon white wine vinegar

½ cup milk

muffin tray

THE GLAZE

1 cup cream

125 g butter

½ cup brandy

½ cup sugar

The magic is really in this glaze - it's the glisten that adds the sparkle to this timeless gem. Melt all the ingredients together and keep warm. When the pud comes out of the oven, pour the glaze over the hot baked Malva Muffins immediately so that it penetrates right through them. Serve individually with double thick whipped cream and/or a scoop of homemade vanilla ice cream. The contrast of piping hot and ice cold is really lekker. (**See page 113 for ice cream recipe.**)

PS. It's best to serve the pudding hot as soon as it comes out of the oven, although at the restaurant where I worked so many years ago I used to sneak into the cold room and eat cold portions. One thing I can promise - try this one and you'll be an addict for ever.

About two hours up the west coast from Cape Town, and just around the corner from the little fishing village of Paternoster, you'll spot the lighthouse on the headland at Cape Columbine. The reserve owes its name to the barque Columbine, which was wrecked along this notorious coastline almost 180 years ago. The same cold and treacherous Benguela current that wreaks such havoc is kind enough to offer up the plumpest black mussels and Cape rock lobster - the bedrock for this delectable festive feast I'm about to share with you.

SEAFOOD PAELLA

Alternative Christmas Holiday Fare // Way down south it really seems crazy to serve up heavy, hot roast dinners with all the trimmings in the middle of our scorching summers. I think a much better idea for Christmas kos is to take advantage of our knockout local produce, like plump black mussels and Mozambican prawns. It's time to break with the meat and potato brigade and rustle up a light and tasty seafood paella instead. Of course you don't have to wait for Christmas; you can make this anywhere any time - just as soon as you've gathered the gang and the ingredients.

★ ★ ★ ★   THIS RECIPE SERVES 6 TO 8   ★ ★ ★ ★ ★

With a dish like this that has so many layers, timing is key. So if you decide to be a maverick and add or leave out a little here and there just be mindful that some ingredients take longer to cook than others. It's great if you have a two handled paellera pan but any shallow pan will do the trick - as long as it's big enough to take the quantity you want to make. If it's not, just use more than one.

① How To Clean Prawns / Rock Lobster
Pull off the head, then on the back of the prawn, slice open the tail and remove the dark thin line of the guts. This is called de-veining.

② How To Clean Mussels
Soak the mussels in a bucket of sea water, preferably overnight. This will allow them to spit out the sand and grit inside their shells. Next day, using a small sharp knife, scrape the mussels clean of all barnacles and other parasites living on the shell. Pull out the beard on the side where it pokes out *(the fibrous connections that attach the mussel to the rock)* and scrape this clean.

YOU'LL NEED TO GET YOUR HANDS ON

3 - 4 Cape rock lobsters

20 West Coast black mussels
  - cleaned, and de-bearded

12 to 18 queen prawns

½ kg firm white fish *- filleted and cubed (Kabeljou's good) and ask your fishmonger to give you the bones for stock*

300 g calamari cut into rings

Marinade for prawns and fish:

1 tablespoon brown sugar

juice of 1 lime

a splash of soya sauce

a good lashing of sesame oil

3 cloves of garlic - *chopped*

a hand of ginger
 - *peeled and chopped*

3 chillies
 - *chopped, seeds and all*

You'll also need:

a pinch of saffron

a handful of parsley

a glass of decent dry
 white wine

olive oil

2-3 cups of Basmati rice

4 cloves of garlic - *chopped*

2 onions - *roughly chopped*

2 hot chillies - *chopped*

6 ripe tomatoes - *quartered*

a few sprigs of rosemary

fish stock

a handful of mangetout

a handful of broad beans

1 red and 1 yellow pepper
 - *seeded and cut into strips*

2 punnets brown mushrooms

2 punnets hand crushed
 oyster mushrooms

6 chorizo sausages (*or any
 other smoked sausage*)

a lemon or two

FIRST UP clean and devein the prawns and rock lobster, keeping their heads and half the shells for the stock. Roast them in the oven for about 10 minutes - this will really bring out their flavour. Marinate the prawns, along with the fish, in a mixture of brown sugar, lime juice, soya sauce, sesame oil, chopped garlic, ginger and chilli. Start making the stock by tossing the prawn and rock lobster heads and shells and fish bones into a pot with a little more water than is required for cooking the rice - this way you will allow for liquid loss while making the stock. Let the stock simmer, not boil.

NEXT toss the mussels and clams into a pot, add a pinch of saffron threads, break up the parsley and add, pour over a glass of wine and give the pot a good shake. Put the lid on and steam until the mussels open, as soon as this happens, remove from the heat. Discard any mussels that haven't opened, as they were probably dead when you picked them and could give you seafood poisoning. Retain the juice at the bottom of the pot - it's full of salty sea flavour and you can add some of this to the fish stock. But be sure to strain before use and add only a little at a time and then taste - it could easily get too savoury!

To tenderise the calamari - moer it with any heavy object you have to hand; this is a sure-fire way of ensuring it stays soft and succulent. Splash olive oil into the pan and quickly fry the prawns and fish to seal. Remove and set aside. Be sure to cover them - remember flies are free and plentiful in Africa. Now fry the rice, the garlic, the onions and the chillies over a medium heat in 6 tablespoons of olive oil (*or as much as it takes to coat the rice thoroughly*), stirring occasionally until the rice goes nice and translucent - the process is similar to Risotto. Then add the calamari, tomatoes, rosemary, and stock. Seal the dish with tin foil, and allow it to cook until the rice is almost done. You can do this either in an oven at 180°C, or on a fire at low heat.

Remove the tinfoil (*keep it in one piece because you're going to use it again*) and drop the following into the rice: half of the mangetout, broad beans, peppers, both kinds of mushrooms, and all the fish, prawns and mussels. Seal again and put back on the heat until the rice is cooked. You're allowed to peek every now and then and taste as well - this is one of the perks of being the officer in charge. You may need to add more stock. Just before you dish up add the remainder of the vegetables - they'll give the paella a lovely fresh crunch - and the chorizo sausage. Season to taste, give it all a good toss and serve immediately with a squeeze of lemon juice.

Important: Don't stir the rice while it's cooking - you'll destroy the channels that help the flavour of the stock to permeate the grains. Remember, too, to check the instructions on the packet with regard to rice vs liquid quantities. I use 1 cup rice to 1½ cups liquid, but it might differ from brand to brand.

Saffron is intrinsic to paella. It comes from southwest Asia and has been known for decades as the world's most expensive spice by weight. This is because it is hand harvested from the flower of the saffron crocus of which only the style and the three stigmas are dried and used. It adds a very distinctive rich golden-yellow tint to this dish, but its flavour is really quite mild.

ROBBEN
ISLAND

REEDOM

"We want Robben Isla
triumph of freedom

I chose to make this recipe at the end of the second season of filming. It was passed on to me by Roshni, after her mom had passed it on to her, when we were filming on the historically significant beach on Robben Island. It's a meal fit for kings and seemed like a fitting tribute to the father of our nation who spent so many years far from his nearest and dearest on this desolate piece of real estate.

MOM'S CRAB CURRY

✦ ✦ ✦ ✦ **THIS RECIPE SERVES 4** ✦ ✦ ✦ ✦

Probably your biggest challenge with this recipe will be to get hold of fresh crabmeat, which many will tell you is the sweetest shellfish of them all. Our local *Scylla serrata*, the mud or mangrove crab, should theoretically be easy to find burrowing away in the mudbanks of estuaries all the way from Knysna through the Eastern Cape and as far up as northern KwaZulu-Natal. But these muddy crustaceans like playing hard to get. So if you're out there looking, keep your ear to the ground and your eyes on the locals - and pinch their secret spot if you can. If you do see anyone who's caught more than a couple, be prepared to barter your wife or girlfriend, or maybe both - it could prove well worth the swap!

In a large pot heat the oil and braise the cinnamon, cardamom, star anise, curry leaves, garlic and onion until the onion is transparent. Keeping the temperature low, add the masala and turmeric and stir. Add all the tomatoes, sugar, salt and half the coriander and simmer until the oil rises to the surface of the sauce. Now toss in the rest of the coriander, saving a little for garnishing. Add butter and chillies and stir. Finally add the crabs to the sauce, making sure they are submerged, bring to the boil and then simmer for about 20 minutes. That's it - tuck in!

All families have certain recipes embedded in their psyches - a sort of gastronomic genetic imprint. These aren't necessarily local and often originate from unexpected quarters - that's the beauty of being part of a rainbow nation. Boerewors came from the French Huguenots and pap from Scotland. Curry spices definitely arrived with the Indians, or was it the Cape Malays? Kanpur or Kuala Lumpur - does it really matter? Like Madiba, they belong to all of us now.

YOU NEED

1 big pot

4 large crabs

For the curry sauce:

3 tablespoons oil

2 cinnamon sticks

4 cardamom pods

4 star anise

a bunch of curry leaves

4 cloves garlic - *chopped*

1 large onion - *sliced*

3 tablespoons masala

2 teaspoons turmeric *(borrie)*

4 very ripe medium-sized tomatoes

415g puréed tomatoes

1½ tablespoons sugar

salt to taste

a bunch of fresh coriander - *use as much or as little as you like*

2 good tablespoons butter

6 hot chillies

Spices add variety to life, so find a local dealer with a decent selection of fresh stock. Cardamom is just about as dear as saffron and quite difficult to find. If you get hold of the pods bruise them before tossing them into your pot, or peel off the skin and just add the seeds - whole or ground. (The name means 'blameless and without reproach' - like Cleopatra when she used their scent to lure Mark Antony to her boudoir. Might be a thought to serve this dish next time you're hoping to score?) Star anise is quite popular at present, but it's always been an integral part of garam masala and traditional Chinese five-spice powder. It has the same distinctive liquorice flavour as the similarly named but unrelated anise, and is often used instead of this pricier spice in liquors like Galliano, Sambuca, Pastis and even in certain brands of Absinthe.

Less than 20 kilometres from the centre of Cape Town, and known affectionately to the locals as 'jija-letwa', this township has overcome many hurdles and is now finally living up to its name, which means 'our pride'. There is a lively sense of community with cultural tours of the township, popular restaurants and hospitable B&Bs. But, hey, don't take my word for it - check it out for yourself.

UMQOMBOTHI

Yvonne Chaka Chaka's song tells how this magic beer makes her people smile and dance. This very talented lady captures the spirit of this indigenous drink beautifully, but I'm not sure that the first glass of traditional sorghum beer will have quite this effect on the uninitiated. I've heard it described as 'a nasty, sour, yeasty tasting liquid'. It's not that it's particularly strong, but seasoned lager or ale drinkers will find it rather flat and a little more yeasty, thick and gritty than their palates are accustomed to. Let's just say it takes some getting used to.

***Umqombothi** is produced commercially but the really authentic stuff is served from large nondescript plastic bottles which have been filled by women who, as the song goes, wake up early every morning and work hard every day to make sure the fire burns to make their special umqombothi - African beer.*

***Give it a try** - it'll grow on you and, given how much cheaper it is than other beer, some of us might just feel the need to acquire the taste. And, who knows, it could just improve our rhythm.*

TRADITIONAL METHOD OF PREPARATION ★★★★

INGREDIENTS

1 kg maize meal
4 kg corn sorghum
tap water

① Chuck the maize meal into a 5 litre bucket and add 1 litre of cold water. Mix and then add a litre of boiling water and leave to cool. When it's reached room temperature, add 2 kg of corn sorghum, stir and leave overnight.
② Next day boil 3 litres of water in a large pot. Add half the previous night's mixture and stir. Bring to the boil, stop stirring and leave to simmer for about half an hour or so. Then pour into a large plastic basin and repeat the process with the remainder of the mixture. Combine the two mixtures and leave to rest.
③ Much later in the day add the remaining 2 kg of corn sorghum and mix thoroughly. Be true to the recipe and use your hands to do this. Once mixed properly cover with an old blanket or sheet and leave in a warm part of your house overnight.

To test if it's ready, light a match close to the vat and when the carbon dioxide fumes kill the flame quickly, the beer is ready. Preferably do this outside. You want to make beer, not burn the house down.

Filter through a large metal strainer and feed the excess corn to your chickens. Now this is an excellent way to treat free-range chicks, don't you think!

Lastly, invite your friends and family over for a tasting. Traditionally, they're expected to show their gratitude by bringing a bottle of brandy to the party. Works for me!

Can you imagine anything more idyllic than spending a spring weekend with 19 mates lazing on a houseboat moored on the tranquil lagoon at Langebaan on the West Coast? Langebaan is one of a series of quaint historic villages which include Lambert's Bay, Paternoster and Saldanha Bay. In case you've never been there, it's about an hour's drive from Cape Town.

SNOEK

Around these parts snoek *(a member of the snake mackerel family)*, mussels and crayfish are staple food, and in August and September the surrounding fields are carpeted with flowering wild daisies, succulents and other brightly coloured fynbos.

Human footprints dating back about 117 000 years have been found on the shore of the lagoon and for nearly as long 'bokkoms', which are salted mullets strung up in bunches and left to dry, have been a local delicacy. In fact the locals regard all the fruits of the ocean as culinary treasures and at the drop of a hat will slap the day's catch on the braai and sit back with a glass of something not so soft and take in the sun sinking slowly over the sea. I was more than happy to join in this quaint custom but first I needed to prepare the side dishes . . .

① **Stuffed Butternuts, Potatoes and Sweet Potatoes on the Braai**
Wash all the veggies well and pat dry. Halve and de-pip the bulb of the butternuts, then fill the cavities with blanched and chopped spinach, feta, butter and parsley. Rub oil and salt on the outside of the potatoes then wrap all the veggies in tin foil and braai on the coals, turning the potatoes regularly for an all over tan. You'll know the butternuts are cooked when the sides squash in easily and the potatoes when a sharp knife slides through them with ease.

② **Strawberry Dressing for a Green Salad**
Place halved strawberries in a bowl. Add 2 tablespoons sugar, balsamic vinegar and chillies to taste. Mix and allow to stand so that the juice from the berries is drawn out and forms a thick syrup which goes beautifully with the snoek. Serve over an array of salad greens, especially peppery rocket.

③ **Snoek on the Braai** Cut the snoek open along the backbone, from the tail to the head. Remove entrails and head and rinse. Next, cut one incision down the centre of each fillet *(be careful not to cut through the skin)*. This increases the surface area of the fish, and what you are left with are two butterflied halves. Down in the Cape this vigorous form of gutting and butterflying a snoek is called 'vlekking'. Whack with salt and allow to stand for 20 minutes. Rinse and pat dry.
Melt a large knob of butter in a saucepan, then add a handful of roughly chopped chillies *(seeds & all)*, a couple of chopped garlic cloves and apricot jam to taste. Combine all ingredients thoroughly. Liberally rub the sweet and sticky marinade/glaze well into the flesh side of fish - be careful because the bones are prickly! It's best to do this once it's on the braai. Place flesh side down on medium heat - that is, when you can hold your hand over the coals for about 8 seconds before it gets too hot. Watch the butter and jam turn golden brown. Then turn fish over to skin side but don't leave too long - allow for about 4 - 5 minutes per side
Get stuck in, but watch out for those bones.

RAVIOLI STUFFED WITH MUSSELS

★ ★ ★ ★ ★   THIS RECIPE SERVES 4   ★ ★ ★ ★ ★

① **STEAMED MUSSELS FOR THE FILLING** Drop the mussels into a pot and break a handful of parsley over them. Pour over the wine and stir well, replace the lid and steam over a medium heat for a few minutes. Take a peek now and then. As soon as the mussels open remove the pot from the heat. Discard any that haven't opened, as they were probably dead when you picked them. Retain the juice at the bottom of the pot. It's full of flavour, so strain it and add it to your tomato sauce a little at a time.

② **HOMEMADE TOMATO SAUCE** *(next page)*

③ **FRESH PASTA** Place the flour on a clean flat surface and make a well in the middle. Break the eggs into the centre of the well and, using your *(clean)* fingers, gently mix the egg into the flour. Once the egg has been absorbed knead the dough for about 10 minutes - pretend it's play dough and have some fun, just don't drop it on the floor! Wrap it in cling wrap and refrigerate for about 20 minutes. If you want a richer dough, use just the yolks from 3 eggs, instead of the 2 whole eggs.

④ **FAT IS FLAVOUR** In the meanwhile cut off a decent stuk of room temperature butter - mix it thoroughly in a bowl with a couple of finely chopped cloves of garlic and some parsley. For those of you who, like me, are partial to the tingle of fire on their tongues, make a second bowl with the same ingredients, but this time add a few chopped chillies.

You'll need

20 fresh black mussels
a glass of dry white wine
a large bunch of fresh parsley
a large knob of butter

fresh pasta...
2 cups flour
2 eggs *(free range or organic)*

⑤ **MAKE THE RAVIOLI**
Sprinkle some flour on your work surface to prevent the dough from sticking. Using your hands, make balls about the size of golf balls; put them through the pasta machine on its thickest setting through to its thinnest, until you have the desired thickness. This will give you a long, flat, broad piece of raw pasta, roughly 3 mm thick. Cut this into squares - 3 fingers x 3 fingers. Place small spoonfuls of flavoured butter and a steamed mussel in the centre of each. Fold into triangles: using your finger, start from the corner and gently push the edge down easing out any air in the pockets. Pinch the edges with a fork to make sure that the ravioli don't explode into a soggy watery mess when you cook them. Repeat until all the filling has been used up.

Drop the ravioli gently into a pot of salty boiling water. Cook until al dente - this'll only take a couple of minutes so keep your eye on these guys. Drain, plate and smother with your rich tomato sauce. Serve with generous shavings of Parmesan and lashings of good olive oil.

If all you've ever done in your life is boil water, it would be a good idea to learn to make this simple sauce before you learn anything else. It'll stand you in good stead with many recipes in this book - and, in fact, throughout your future culinary life.

HOMEMADE TOMATO SAUCE

In a pan, fry the garlic and onion in the olive oil and butter until the onions are clear and have softened. Add the fresh and canned tomatoes. Break up the anchovies with your fingers and add them. Lastly add the strained juice from the steamed mussels in the previous recipe, a little at a time, tasting before adding more. Let this all simmer, not boil, for about half an hour until the fresh tomatoes have disintegrated into the sauce. If you prefer a thicker sauce, allow to simmer with the lid off for 10 minutes or so before serving.

Ouma's Trick: If the sauce is too acidic for you, add a pinch or two of sugar to make it mellow out.

You'll need

2 cloves of garlic
 - peeled and roughly chopped

1 peeled white onion
 - thinly sliced

3-4 tablespoons olive oil

knob of butter

4 vine-ripened plum tomatoes *- roughly chopped, skin and all*

1 tin whole peeled tomatoes

2 anchovy fillets

TARZAN ROAST

In the upper reaches of the majestic Olifants River Valley this hideaway on stilts in the middle of a poplar forest brought out the primeval male in me and I was tempted to swing from the branches and yell . . . FIRE! About two million years ago, somewhere along the southern tip of Africa, man discovered quite by chance that ripping off large hunks of meat and chucking them in the flames did startling things to the flavour. From that day forward the heat's been on and no dassie or duiker, eland or elephant or any other four-legged herbivore, wild or domestic, has escaped a roasting. We've developed a myriad of hot variations and every red-blooded male has an arsenal of braai techniques. I, too, have a few strings to my bow but once in a while I'm forced to admit that another guy's idea is a killer. This one goes to Braam Kruger in whose amazing book Provocative Cuisine I first discovered this primordial method - he calls it Tarzan Roast . . . and, by Jane, it rocks! You may recognise it by its ancient name - a Poacher's Roast.

Lay the leg of lamb on its side in the baking tray and, using a small sharp knife, cut slits 3-5 cm deep at a 45 degree angle all over the lamb. Force rosemary sprigs, chilli and garlic slivers into the slits, then dip the spring onions in the oyster sauce and force them in as well - the green leaves will jut out, a bit like a porcupine! Mix together the oregano, the balance of the oyster sauce, the onions and the juice from the lemons and orange, and pour this all over the leg of lamb. Leave to marinate while you make the fire in the wheelbarrow.

COOKING METHOD The meat actually cooks by radiated heat and is gently smoked at the same time. I usually use orange or apple wood because of their aromatic properties and I make the fire in a wheelbarrow. This is useful because the cooking time is somewhere between 4 and 6 hours, and during that period of time Mother Nature could blow hot and cold and change her tune a number of times. But with a wheelbarrow you can adjust the position of the fire and take full advantage of the prevailing wind.

READY TO COOK First, slip the wire through the shank and twist it so there's no chance of the meat falling into the fire. Attach the wire to the rope with a slipknot.

THE TREE Once the leg is attached to the wire and the rope you need to find a nice strong branch in a tall tree from which to hang your meat. *(Be sure that it's far enough away from your house and any dry tinder. You don't want to end up chasing a runaway fire.)* Again using a slipknot attach the rope to the branch and then, between the wire and the tree, make a sheepshank knot in the rope - this way, you can adjust the height of the lamb as required. Balance the baking tray with the left over marinade on a stool and position this directly under the joint. Wheel the fire in next to the stool and place it so that the prevailing wind is blowing towards the lamb. You should be able to hold your hand between the fire and meat for just a few seconds without burning it. If it's not hot enough chuck a couple of extra logs on the fire to really get the heat going. You can use the forked stick to push the leg closer or further from the heat. And that's it. For the next 4 to 6 hours, you need to keep basting the lamb with marinade and the fatty juices that drip into the tray. Every 10 to 15 minutes turn the meat about 45 degrees and secure its position with the forked stick.

INGREDIENTS

You will need

about a 3 ½ kg fatty leg of lamb, with the shank intact *- very important*

a few sprigs of rosemary

a couple of whole chillies *- as hot as you can handle*

10-15 cloves of garlic *- peeled and cut in half*

3-4 bunches of spring onions

¼ cup oyster sauce

a handful of dried oregano

2 onions *- sliced*

the juice of 2 to 3 lemons

the juice of 1 orange

. . . as well as . . .
a baking tray

about half a metre of galvanised wire

2-3 metres of rope

a forked stick

a basting brush

a sharp knife

a small stool

a wheelbarrow *- useful for both braaiing and gardening*

orange wood *- any hard fruit wood will do, but do not use ordinary firewood*

an accessible branch on a tree that is not too close to your house

VERY IMPORTANT: Keep testing the heat and adding a log when necessary. Otherwise, your early evening meal could turn into a midnight feast.

Slip Knot

Sheepshank Knot (ironic)

While you're rolling the joint and smoking it . . .

We were fortunate enough to make our manly meal in the Cederberg where there was plenty of space to let off steam, but if you're not lucky enough to be able to get out into the great outdoors don't despair, take a stab at it wherever you may be. Just remember this macho way of cooking a hefty hunk of lamb takes mega time and if you hit the jungle juice and form a laager with a lager too early things could get really hairy.

One way of avoiding this is to take some time out to get in touch with your sensitive side.

Include the ladies and absorb the bits of nature that suburbia has on offer. First up, turn on your sprinkler *(it's good for cooling off any coals that sneak out of the braai)*, but just long enough to get the lawn damp enough to bring out the earthworms which will attract the birds. Then take off those boots - being kaalvoet so that the mud can squelch between your toes is essential. Now get down and do some sky gazing. Encourage your mates to join you as this is an excellent time to get your lawn weeded. I'm not prescribing total abstinence - basking while

sipping slowly from Bohemian glass goblets *(or cracking a can, if you must)* gets the mind juices flowing and leads to some beautiful banter. Be on the lookout for birdcalls, butterflies and bugs. Just don't forget to turn your meat!

After 4 hours or so of chilling, poke a skewer into the thickest section of the joint to see if it's cooked. If the juices ooze out red, it's still raw and needs more cooking; pink juices mean the meat is perfectly medium rare. When it is cooked, raise the leg or remove the heat and let it rest for ten minutes.

SERVING SUGGESTIONS

I normally carve the meat while it is still hanging up - that way, if it's a bit too rare closer to the bone, you can just drop the roast back near the heat and cook it for a bit longer. So, finally, you've got this pile of perfectly smoked lamb and a group of ravenous mates. Now what?

Option ① - Hands On
Grab pita bread. Slice open to make a pocket. Stuff with shredded lettuce, roughly chopped tomato, fresh basil, medium rare lamb and a good dollop of Greek yoghurt. *Don't wait . . . get stuck in!*

Option ② - Serve with Root Veggies Start preparing at about the 3-hour mark. Chop all the veggies into pieces about the same size so that they will all be ready at the same time. *Use: baby potatoes, beetroot, parsnips, carrots, sprigs of rosemary, olive oil.*

Preheat the oven to 180°C. Blanch the various vegetable types separately in boiling salted water for 10 minutes. Place on a baking tray, add the rosemary and drizzle with olive oil. Slow roast for between 40 minutes and 1 hour, turning occasionally. Once they're cooked, reduce the heat of the oven to its lowest setting to keep them warm.

While the roast is resting make a sauce by pouring all the drippings and scraps of lamb in the baking tray into a pan, mix a teaspoon of cornflour in a cup of milk and add this to the pan. Keep stirring on low heat for between 5 to 10 minutes until the sauce begins to thicken. To serve, place vegetables and slivers of roast lamb on a platter and drizzle the sauce over the meat. *No need to stand on ceremony - help yourself!*

These sweet treats can be made in two ways. The recipe below is for what we call the boere koeksister, and evidence that the Afrikaners regard this as a national treasure is the two-metre high statue of one erected in their enclave of Orania - unusual, to say the least! Then there is the Cape Malay 'koesuster', which looks and tastes quite different. This is more of a bun that's flavoured with ginger, cinnamon and cardamom, cooked in citrus-flavoured syrup and sprinkled with desiccated coconut. They both have devoted followers and it would be a declaration of war for me to take sides. What I will say is that both are weapons of dietary destruction, so enjoy but know that you'll have to pay the price, or hit the road - take a long brisk walk or, better yet, get jogging!

KOEKSISTERS

INGREDIENTS

For the dough you'll need:

240 g cake flour

4 teaspoons baking powder

½ teaspoon of salt

2 tablespoons of butter

½ cup of sour milk or buttermilk

For the syrup you'll need:

1 kg sugar

2 cups of water

¼ teaspoon cream of tartar

a pinch of salt

grated peel and juice of

1 lemon (*avoid the pith - it has a rather bitter taste*)

1 hand of bruised, peeled ginger

To deep-fry you'll need:

canola oil - which I prefer as it's reasonably priced, good at high heat, and it's the healthier option

★ ★ ★ ★ **THIS MAKES ABOUT ENOUGH** ★ ★ ★ ★

① Sift the dry ingredients together and rub in the butter. Add the sour milk (*or buttermilk*) and mix into a soft dough; knead thoroughly, then leave to stand for about 15 minutes.

② Chuck all the syrup ingredients into a saucepan. Heat and stir until all the sugar is dissolved. Simmer for a few minutes, then remove from the heat and chill (*stick it into freezer for a while to get really cold*). By now your dough should be perfect for plaiting. Roll out to a thickness of about 5mm and cut into strips 5 mm wide and about 7 cm long. Create plaits with three strips, making sure that you press the strips together firmly at both ends - this is very important because if you don't, the koeksister will fall apart in the oil.

③ Deep fry the koeksisters in hot oil until golden brown - think crunchy outside, but not burnt. Drain quickly and immediately dip into the ice-cold syrup. The trick is to have the koeksisters as hot as possible and the syrup as cold as possible because this way they absorb the syrup better. Once they're saturated remove and leave to set on a wire drying rack.

Take a bite and let the syrup run down your chin. For pure hedonism I like to dip them in freshly whipped cream. But then I'm not counting calories.

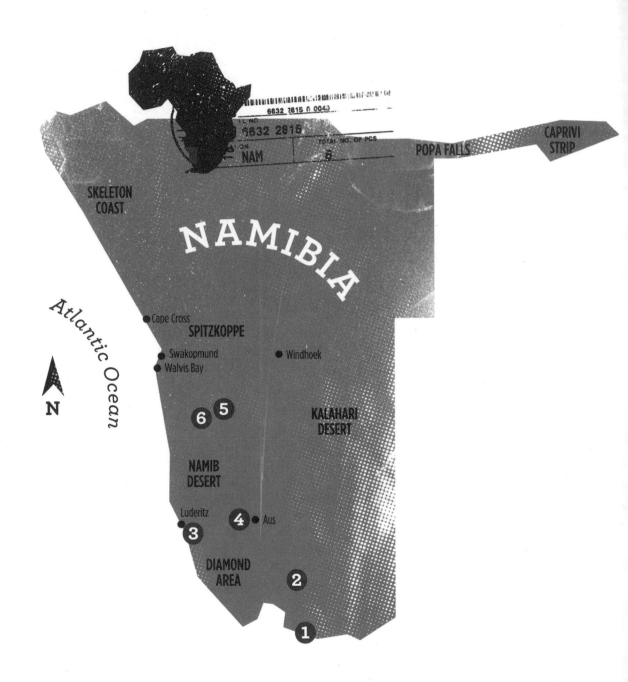

SKELETON
COAST

NAMIBIA

POPA FALLS

CAPRIVI
STRIP

● Cape Cross

SPITZKOPPE

● Swakopmund
● Walvis Bay

● Windhoek

6 **5**

KALAHARI
DESERT

NAMIB
DESERT

Luderitz
●
3

4 ● Aus

DIAMOND
AREA

2

1

Atlantic Ocean

N

6632 2815 0 0040

6632 2815

NAM   6

DESERTS

For centuries people have used pit ovens for cooking out of doors. It's nothing more than the slow, even release of heat within a sealed hole in the earth and things cooked this way stay juicy and flavoursome. Since no flame or fire ever reaches the food, there's no danger of it burning. You should think of this as an underground slow steam cooker.

BUILDING A PIT OVEN

To get started, you need a whole load of igneous rocks, the kind used in a sauna. Metamorphic and sedimentary rocks contain water and will explode when heated and you'll be pulling shrapnel out of your mates' backsides *(or worse)*.

1. Gather a whole lot of fist-size igneous rocks.
2. Dig a hole approximately three times the size of the food you're going to cook. Keep the soil to use later.
3. Line the bottom and sides of the hole with the smaller rocks.
4. Make a fire in the pit with lots of wood and charcoal.
5. Once the fire is burning well build a pyramid of rocks around it.
6. Let the fire burn down until the rocks collapse - this will take a while.

TIP *If you don't remember your school geography, igneous rocks are formed by the solidification of cooled magma (molten rock). A simple - but not foolproof - test is to bash two rocks together. If they're igneous, they'll generally make a ringing sound.*

a large knob of butter

fresh rosemary or
tarragon sprigs - *if you're*
making two chickens, try one
of each

black pepper and Maldon
sea salt to taste

2 lemons

12 washed banana leaves

TIPS

When cooking bigger animals *in your pit oven, it's advisable to cut the meat into a number of smaller pieces so it'll cook faster and more thoroughly. For some reason vegetables take longer than normal, so parboil them before chucking them in the pit oven.*

Since the cooking process relies on steam and not dry heat, green plant material is needed to create the steam. For the herb layer you can use any edible leaves except cabbage - these impart their flavour to whatever you're cooking. So be creative!

Estimating the time *it takes to cook the food depends on so many variables, but here are some rough guidelines. A chicken takes between 2 and 3 hours, a whole pig will take 6 to 8 hours. Leave for longer rather than less time. If you don't get it right first time, you'll have to finish your meal off on the braai or in the oven, but it's unlikely to come to this.*

Rosemary *is that woody perennial with thick needle-like evergreen leaves that give off a strong fragrance when you rub them. It's pretty hardy and easy to grow and if there isn't a bush in your garden you should scout around because there's bound to be one in the neighbourhood. Try to get to know the person who owns it but if that's not possible then it's midnight raid time. Break off a few pieces and plant in full sun at dusk or dawn, water it well immediately and soon you'll be the one guarding your crop.*

PIT OVEN CHICKEN

Make a flavoured butter by pulling the rosemary or tarragon leaves from their stems and tossing them into a bowl with the butter, black pepper and sea salt. Use a fork to mash all these ingredients together thoroughly. Slide a finger in between the skin and the meat on top of the chicken breast and create a pocket, then push the flavoured butter into the pocket and massage the bird to make sure the butter is spread evenly under the skin. Drizzle the juice from one lemon all over the chicken. Cut the second lemon in two and pop it into the cavity. The metro-man method is then to dress the chicken in a double layer of tin foil, which works fine but is not nearly as inventive nor as primal as wrapping it in five layers of banana leaves and securing these with a piece of wire or butcher's string. The chicken cooks in its own moisture and the aromas from the green herbs get in everywhere - leaving you with a truly lekker hoender.

TO COOK THE CHICKEN

1. Splash a bit of water on to the stones - they should be so hot that the water evaporates instantly - think of pouring water on to sauna rocks. If they're not hot enough, add more wood.
2. Using a pair of tongs, remove the top layer of rocks. Leave the bottom layer but remove any remaining burning coals.
3. Place three banana leaves on the bottom layer of rocks, followed by a bunch of edible green plants or herbs. More rosemary or tarragon will do nicely.
4. Place the wrapped chicken on top of the herbs.
5. Cover with more herbs and/or the remaining banana leaves, then pile on the hot rocks. Cover these with an old towel or piece of fabric to keep the sand out.
6. Lastly - fill in the hole with the soil and walk away.

It's going to take between 2 and 3 hours for the chicken to cook, but rather err on the side of caution and only take it out after 3 hours. It's impossible to burn your chicken and the longer it cooks, the more likely the meat is to fall off the bone. Just be careful not to get sand in your dinner. This is a primitive method of cooking and so it's only fitting that it's eaten South African style - with your fingers. Try out a small pit oven and do a chicken. When you've built up your confidence go huge and cook a whole lamb or even a pig.

We set out for our road trip to Namibia in a fancy overland vehicle and our first stop came soon after we'd crossed the border. While pitching the tents we could gaze down on the majestic Orange River that has been flowing westwards to the sea for millennia. While we were looking forward to the morning when we would be on the water paddling with the flow, it'd been a long day's travelling and some R & R was definitely in order. But first the gang needed sustenance, so we got stuck in preparing a supper high in carbos so that everybody would be up and firing on all cylinders at first light the next morning.

WORS
CANNELLONI

What's better after a long day than a hearty pasta and no matter how tired you are there is no excuse for not making it fresh. Not even leaving half the pasta machine at home stopped us from 'maaking 'n plan' and producing the goods.

Carbo-load and be happy, for tomorrow you might have to face the rapids!

① **See how to make pasta on page 37** then turn it in to cannelloni by cutting it into 7cm strips and parboiling them.

② Fry up some boerewors and make a white sauce **(see page 102 for making a roux)** and a tomato sauce **(see page 39)** to which you add a handful of capers.

③ Line a baking dish with the white sauce then roll the pieces of sausage in the pasta strips and pack them on top. Repeat these till you've filled the dish or you've run out of ingredients. Smother with your rich tomato sauce and grate over stacks of parmesan and Gruyère cheese. Bake in the oven at 180°C for half an hour.

I don't know what it is about wide open spaces but I just love the great outdoors. I'll visit isolated areas anywhere, anytime, anyhow. One of these is the Fish River Canyon in southern Namibia. It's truly one of the natural wonders of Africa and it gives you such a high when you look down over the edge where the earth drops half a kilometre below the Huib Plateau. This boldly beautiful chasm just bellowed for us to explore its rare bare essence.

On the day before we cruised down into the canyon proper, we stopped over on the southwestern edge. From here we could look out at the flat-topped mesas and the 1500-million-year-old exposed rock and earthy colours. Our camp was pitched on the vast plain where zebra and buck, including springbok, have for centuries grazed on the sparse grasslands. In the distance the only links between the earth and the sky were the erect quiver trees, named by the San who used their hollow branches as quivers. It seems as if there's always been an eternal contest between man and beast - our forefathers used arrows, snares and, finally, rifles to hunt for the pot. I wanted to honour the tradition - only difference being that I sourced my meat from a butcher in the area, and the local red wine is a lot better than any of the brews concocted by our ancestors.

I chose springbok neck, which has very little fat and, like all tougher cuts of venison, is best cooked very slowly in a three-legged potjie. Since the Dutch introduced this widely used pot to Africa over 200 years ago it's been used for everything from stews to brews and is also great for breads. Because of this is it affectionately known as the Maluti Mountain microwave. I have a collection of potjies of various sizes and never leave home without at least two on a hot standby.

It was dusk by the time the meal was ready and we relaxed with plenty of good red wine. As the sun set and the canyon burst into flames of scarlet and orange, the silhouettes of the massive aloes stood like sentries guarding our camp. In spite of the vastness of the terrain I felt safe and secure enveloped in the arms of the painted landscape.

There's something a little macabre about cooking the national emblem - our dainty Springbok. This little antelope can run at 80 kilometres an hour and leaps in the air for the pure joy of it. But once you've savoured its distinctive flavour you'll appreciate that this elegant creature has more to offer than speed and agility.

SPRINGBOK NECK POTJIE

WITH DUMPLINGS & A DOUGHBOY

★★★★★ THIS RECIPE SERVES ABOUT 6 ★★★★★

If you can't find springbok or get your head around eating venison, you can substitute with neck of lamb. And if you don't have a potjie you can use any heavy pot with a good tight-fitting lid on a tripod. *(But you really should get at least one potjie.)* If you can't cook on an open fire, you can do this at low heat on a hob, but it isn't nearly as energy efficient and unfortunately the whole experience won't be quite as good.

Ideally potjiekos is cooked in the great outdoors over an open fire, but in winter I use mine inside, next to my fireplace. Potjie pots aren't fussy and you can even burn charcoal. Once the cast iron is well heated it needs just the occasional smoldering log or hot coal under its round belly to keep it sizzling happily and very soon you'll begin to recognise its distinctive whisper - reassurance that comfort food is on the way.

You'll need

about 1½ kg springbok neck
in thick pieces
enough cake flour to coat
the meat
a good dollop of olive oil
1 onion, roughly chopped
3 cloves of garlic
... or as a whole neck
2 teaspoons salt
freshly ground black pepper
to taste
1 sprig of fresh rosemary
250g good red wine
... ...
1 cup beef stock (warmed)
... leeks cut into thin rounds
... big red ... ...

Coat the meat in flour and brown in hot oil in the potjie pot to seal. Remove the meat and set aside. Add the onion and garlic and sauté until the onion is translucent. Reduce the temperature of the pot and add the meat, salt, black pepper, rosemary, wine and stock and give it a good stir, then put on the lid and leave to simmer on gentle heat for 2½ to 3 hours until the meat is tender. It is very important that the dish just simmers (the potjie pot whisper). If the meat boils rapidly it will become tough and taste like old leather so, please, no rushing . . . gentle heat only. When the meat is starting to become tender layer the leeks, carrots and butternut on top of it, without stirring. Replace the lid and cook for a further 20 minutes. Now add the doughboy and the dumplings.

FOR DUMPLINGS AND THE DOUGHBOY

2 teaspoons baking powder
500 g cake flour
big pinch of salt
grated pecorino cheese
large knob of butter
about 1 cup of cold water

Sift the baking powder, salt and flour together. Add the pecorino cheese, and then gently rub in the butter with your clean fingertips. Gradually add cold water until you have a soft dough. To make the doughboy, roll out a piece of dough and cut out or model a gingerbread man and place it on top of the veggies at least half submerged in the gravy in the centre of the pot. Break off small pieces from the rest of the dough *(about half the size of a chicken's egg)* and place around the doughboy. Put the lid on and cook for a further 20 minutes.

Important! // No peeking or the dumplings will flop.

Now dish up, sit back and enjoy with a glass or two of good red wine.

Take good care of your potjie pot and it'll be around for years. After using, wash it thoroughly in hot soapy water and when it's dry rub the inside thoroughly with a little vegetable oil - this will prevent it from rusting.

No. 74

96 6632 2015

2.7

KOLMANSKOP

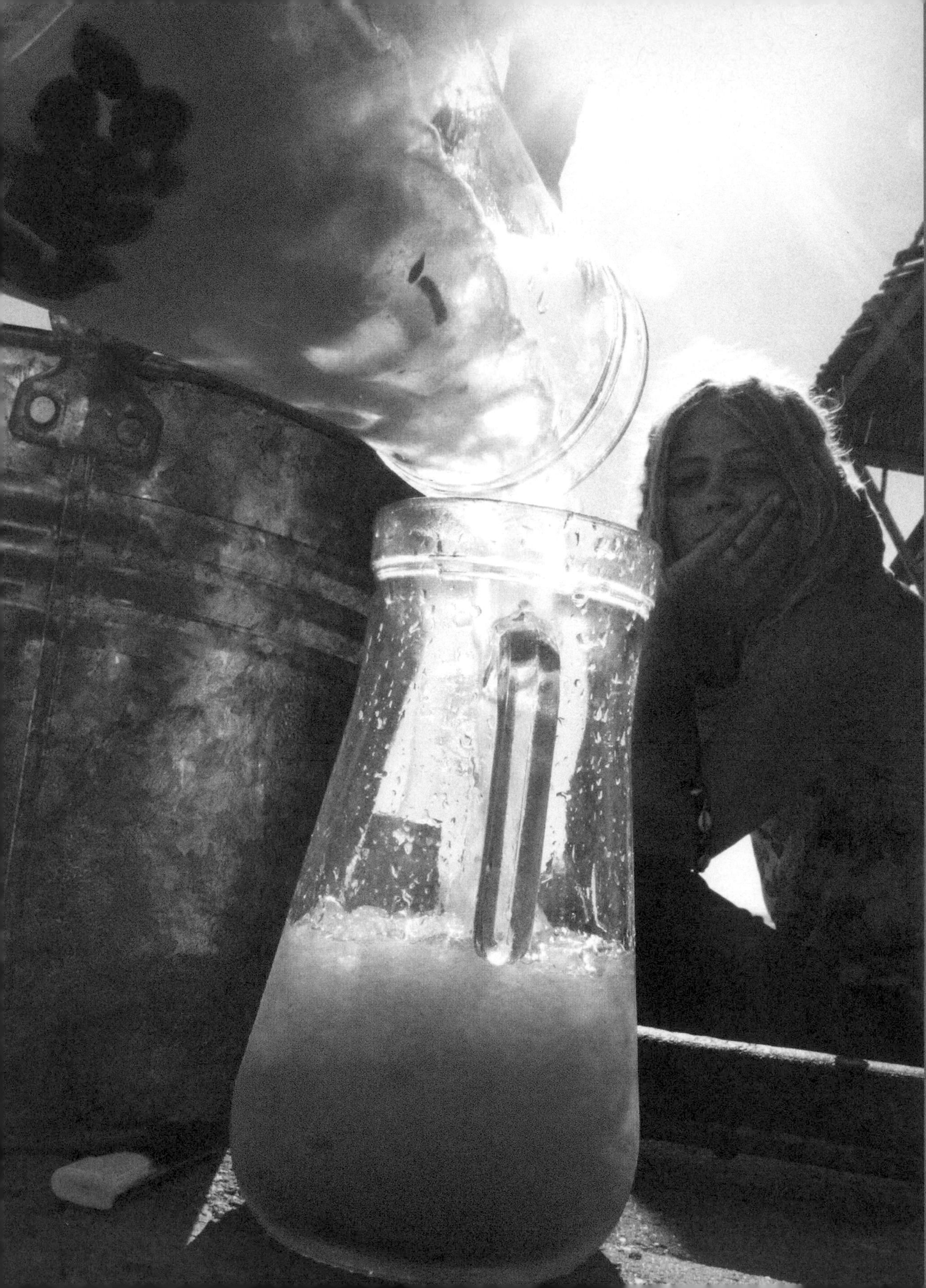

Quite a little gem in its time, this derelict diamond-mining town has turned into a dry gulch. Sadly, even the ice factory no longer operates and we could have done with a ready supply on the day . . .

HOME-MADE LEMONADE

If you ever need something to lift your spirits and wet your whistle, try home-made lemonade. We certainly needed some when we hit the hot and dusty ghost town of Kolmanskuppe and this effervescent drink just hit the spot.

THE TRICK IS TO REMEMBER THE RATIO: 1 cup sugar: 1 cup water: 1 cup of lemon juice (which is roughly 5 lemons). If you prefer it to be less sweet, cut down on the sugar a little.

INGREDIENTS

1 cup sugar - *reduce to ¾ cup if you'd prefer it less sweet*

1 cup water

1 cup lemon juice

a handful of raisins

cold water and ice - *so that you can dilute to taste*

✼ ✼ ✼ ✼ MAKES ABOUT 6 GLASSES ✼ ✼ ✼ ✼

The secret to perfect lemonade is to make a simple syrup by dissolving the sugar in warm water so that it's dispersed evenly instead of sinking to the bottom. So if you have a stove handy, heat the sugar and water in a small saucepan and stir until it's completely dissolved; otherwise just stir very well. Extract the juice from the lemons. I use my Grannie's juicer but you can do this anyway you like. Pour the juice and sugar water into a jug, throw in the raisins and leave for a while, overnight if possible, to allow them to start fermenting and give it a fizz. Before serving add about 2 cups of cold water and a bag of ice to the jug - more or less, depending on how strong you want it to be. If the lemonade is still a little sweet for anyone's taste, chuck a slice or two of lemon into the glass.

The red-sand sea of the Namib is the most diverse desert on earth and Klein Aus Vista offers wild horses, diamonds and dunes - strong medicine that called for a powerful antidote, and I had just the remedy.

SPIKED WATERMELON

If you're squeamish around needles or can't handle hard tack then this operation might not be what the doctor ordered. On the other hand, this potion works wonders for people who don't shy away from the cut and thrust and need a little more than a medicine measure of melon-flavoured balm to raise their spirits.

All it takes is a watermelon, a bottle of vodka and the largest syringe, with needle, that you can find.

The trick is to inject as much vodka as possible into the flesh of the watermelon - don't be afraid, this baby can handle a healthy dose. Jab it all over and if any vodka starts to seep out patch it up with a plaster. Now cool this tonic down, either in the fridge or in a cooler box full of ice - the colder it gets the quicker it'll take effect. When you're feeling up for it, slice off the peel, dig in and heal yourself. Gesondheid!

SOUSSOSVLEI 2,8

THREE BEAN & TOMATO SOUP

Feeds 3 to 4 friends, unless they're starving. If they are, double up the quantities!

WITH SPINACH AND YOGHURT

In a deep pot fry the onions and garlic in the olive oil until they're translucent. Add the cayenne pepper and paprika, give it a good stir and then add the tins of whole peeled tomatoes, the roughly chopped fresh tomatoes and the juice from the 3 tins of beans. Let this simmer on a low heat until the fresh tomatoes disintegrate, then add the beans and simmer for a further 5 minutes.

TO SERVE Put a small layer of spinach in the bottom of a soup bowl, ladle over the soup, and crown with two tablespoons of yoghurt. Flavour with freshly ground pepper, Maldon sea salt and fresh basil. Eat immediately with slices of toasty ciabatta.

PS: For all the meat lovers out there, this soup can easily be turned into a meaty version by simply adding some smoked sausages. I use either Bockwurst, which is a German veal sausage or Chouriço - a cured pork sausage from Portugal. Cut into bite-sized medallions and add along with the beans.

INGREDIENTS

1 onion, roughly sliced

a couple of cloves of garlic
- *peeled and sliced*

a good dollop of olive oil

½ teaspoon cayenne pepper

½ teaspoon Hungarian paprika

2 tins whole peeled tomatoes
(preferably Italian)

8 ripe tomatoes
- *quartered, skin and all*

1 tin garbanzo beans
(chickpeas)

1 tin sugar beans

1 tin butter beans

a bunch of spinach *(or morogo)*
- *stems removed and finely chopped*

500 ml Bulgarian yoghurt

freshly ground black pepper

Maldon sea salt

a small handful of chopped fresh basil

Garbanzo beans are delicious little nutty balls which are a great source of protein, so keep a couple of cans for quick use or buy the dry ones and boil them up yourself. They're used in Middle Eastern and Indian dishes like hummus, falafels and curries. Locally, one usually finds the beige-coloured beans but you can get black, green, red and brown chickpeas too - look out for these because they'll add colour to your cooking.

Maldon sea salt is available at most supermarkets and I always have some in my kitchen. It's a bit more expensive than the local stuff but then it's full of natural trace elements and has the Organic Food Federation's stamp of approval. It's produced by a small family business in Maldon on the east coast of the UK. The crystals break up easily and it has miles more flavour than ordinary table salt. Try a sprinkle - it's good stuff.

Cayenne pepper and Hungarian paprika are two red-hot spices that come from Cayenne in French Guiana and Hungary respectively. The dried and powdered hot chilli pepper from Guiana is every bit as potent as it looks, so use it sparingly. When this is combined with the strong, rich paprika, you'll have a brew so hot you'll be able to serve it outside in July. Buy only a small quantity of each and use them soon or they'll go stale.

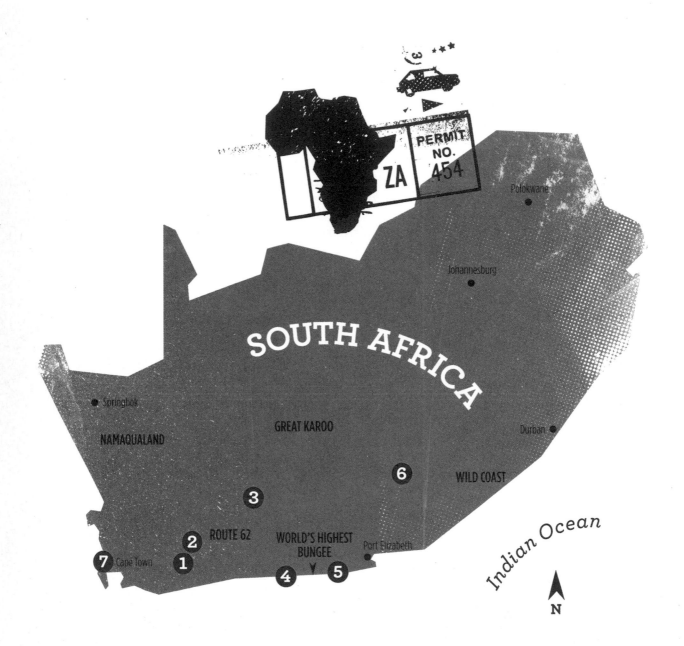

PERMIT NO. ZA 454

SOUTH AFRICA

Polokwane

Johannesburg

Springbok

GREAT KAROO

Durban

NAMAQUALAND

6

WILD COAST

3

Indian Ocean

2 ROUTE 62

WORLD'S HIGHEST
BUNGEE

Port Elizabeth

7 Cape Town

1

4

5

N

ON THE ROAD

ALWAYS TAKE YOUR ITALIAN CAMPING

Getting up at first light is what camping in the bush is all about. Sleeping bags and steamy breath, the smell of wood smoke in your hair and clothes and an enamel mug of good strong coffee in your hand.

Now there's only one way to make a decent stove top espresso on the flames and that's with a MOKA POT BREWER. All you need is a low to medium flame on your gas burner, a little water in the bottom, your special blend of finely ground coffee in the filter basket and in five minutes you'll be sitting pretty sipping proper moer koffie and taking in the sunrise. If you want to be a touch more eagle-eyed and are in need of a sun-upper, add a tot of brandy or a couple of slivers of freshly chopped chilli on top of the ground coffee before putting it on the heat - that's sure to open them blinkers and let the rays stream in! On the other hand, if you're after a mellower awakening, toss in a vanilla pod, a cinnamon stick or a couple of stuks of freshly chopped ginger and let the world unfold slowly before your eyes.

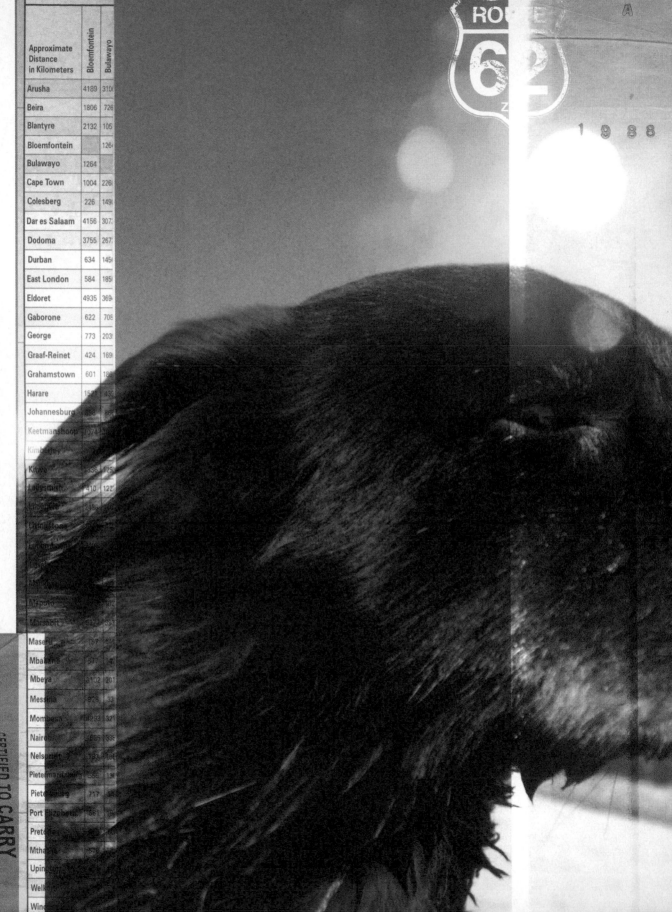

Approximate Distance in Kilometers	Bloemfontein	Bulawayo
Arusha	4189	3100
Beira	1806	726
Blantyre	2132	105
Bloemfontein		1264
Bulawayo	1264	
Cape Town	1004	2260
Colesberg	226	1490
Dar es Salaam	4156	3072
Dodoma	3755	2670
Durban	634	1450
East London	584	1850
Eldoret	4935	3690
Gaborone	622	708
George	773	2030
Graaf-Reinet	424	1690
Grahamstown	601	1880
Harare	1521	435
Johannesburg	398	867
Keetmanshoop	1074	
Kimberley		
Kitwe	2338	1253
Ladysmith	410	1221
Lilongwe	2198	
Livingstone		
Lobatse		
Lusaka		
Mafikeng		
Maputo		802
Marsabit	5172	3853
Maseru	157	
Mbabane	617	
Mbeya	3102	2010
Messina	926	330
Mombasa	5293	3210
Nairobi	4685	3390
Nelspruit	753	
Pietermaritzburg	556	1360
Pietersburg	717	
Port Elizabeth	681	
Pretoria		
Mthatha	576	
Upington		
Welkom		
Windhoek		

ROUTE
62
1988

We've all been on the road and stopped off at one of those 21st century brightly lit roadside spots that flash good food, good pies, good times. We've filled our arms with padkos and hit the road only to discover once again that what we've bought is plastic and not a patch on the home cooking to which we've grown accustomed. I have a simple solution - take some time to prepare your own before you leave home.

PADKOS

★★★★ STUFFED VETKOEK ★★★★

Vetkoek have been on the African kitchen table or cooked in the outdoors since Ma and Pa fell off the wagon. I either stuff them or eat them piping-hot, just cut in half and smeared with butter and a sprinkle of sugar. If you're away from home and have forgotten this recipe, remember that you can make your regular bread dough **(page 207)** because it works just as well. Make them on the road or the night before - you decide if you want them hot or cold!

This recipe makes about 12, depending on how big you make them.

Sieve the flour, add the sugar, salt and yeast and mix well. Make a well in the centre of the flour and add the water a little at a time until the dough starts to pull away from the sides of the mixing bowl. Cover with a tea towel and leave to rise for 20 minutes.

Heat enough oil for deep frying in a pan. The oil must be hot, but not smoking. If you want to make normal vetkoek, drop in a ball of dough and fry until golden brown on all sides. Drain and eat.

If you want to make stuffed vetkoek, it's the same procedure except that you wrap the egg and/or sausage in dough, and then deep fry. It's as simple as that. For those of you with a sweet tooth, try wrapping the dough around a Mars Bar - voila, you've got a really sweet treat.

YOU WILL NEED

1 kg bread flour

1 cup sugar

1 teaspoon salt

10 ml yeast

1 litre lukewarm water

oil for frying - *I use canola because it's healthier*

For the filling

6 boiled eggs - *shelled*

a coil of cooked, thin boerewors - *cut into pieces roughly 3 cm long*

3 days

13 days

6 seconds

17 days

8 hours

More time to enjoy my Rolex . . . My plastic lighter, pinched by James and my heirloom Rolex, originally my dad's, have more in common than you would think. This has nothing to do with their cost and everything to do with their value. No matter how careful one is, during their lifetime they'll pass from one owner to the next: the Rolex because no one is able to hold on to life long enough, and the lighter because no one is able to hold on to it long enough.

23 days

37 days

4 days

52 minutes

19 hours

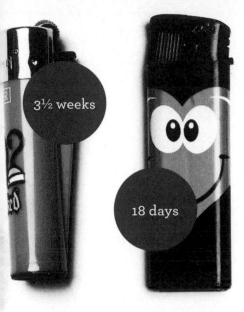

3½ weeks

18 days

1 day

20 hours

243 days

AFRICA

How much I smoke matters to the Rolex because this affects how soon it'll be passed on and how much I smoke matters to the lighter because this affects how soon it'll pass out. I look at it like this . . . I get happy when the lighter moves on or passes out because this means I'll live longer and have more time to enjoy the Rolex before I pass out and it moves on. Wow, look at the time . . . you'll have to excuse me while I pop down to the café to replace another 'lost' lighter.

46 seconds

7 days

43 days

57 minutes

6 days

DRUNKEN BIRDS FOR THE BOYS

When we decided to go on a boys' only fishing weekend in Dutoitskloof the lads said it sounded a little tame so I came up with just the thing to liven things up - a couple of steamy birds.

This is a super simple recipe that combines two of man's favourite pastimes - braaiing and cracking a can. Add 2 juicy chicks and how can it go wrong? Chuck the garlic, pepper and salt into your pestle and mortar and mung the flavours together. Now add a good splash of olive oil and parsley - just bruise the leaves. Use this marinade to give the birds a good old massage all over, inside and out.

When the coals are ready, crack open the beers, take a swig of each and perch the well-oiled birds upright on the open cans, wriggle them down so that they're comfortable and the cavity is filled - we don't want them falling over. Then settle them on the grid and close the Weber. Allow the chickens to cook for between 40 to 80 minutes. The secret here is that the beer boils and steams the flesh from the inside giving it that malty flavour and keeping it juicy while the Weber acts like a braai/oven and crisps the skin.

Who needs other birds when these are so plump and tender!

First off - get the heat up and light a fire in your Weber.

THEN TAKE:

2 whole chickens

2 cans of ale

4 cloves of garlic

whole black pepper corns

Maldon sea salt

olive oil

a small sprig of flat leafed parsley

TOMATO BRUSCHETTA WITH BRANDY FLAMBÉED
SPADE STEAK

This has to be done on a fire for obvious reasons. Take a spade *(not a shovel)* and clean it well to remove all sand and grit and then put it directly on the coals to sterilise. When it's piping hot - you'll know because the shaft will be hot to the touch - rub the fillets in olive oil, then pat thoroughly with the steak rub and place them on the spade. They're going to sizzle - that's the whole idea. Let them cook for about 2 minutes per side - ostrich fillet should be served rare.

Now comes the interesting part. Flambé the steaks by splashing a generous amount of tipple over them. It's going to flare up so stand back and be careful. When the brandy's burnt off, remove the fillets and let them rest for a few minutes so that all the juices are absorbed into the meat before you carve. If you are feeling particularly carnivorous, cut into medallions and chow as is, without the bruschetta and greens.

In the mean time cut the bruschettas in half and toast them on the fire until they're really crispy but not burned. If you don't have a grid, you can toast them on the spade. Once toasted, rub the raw garlic clove over them. This will add a fresh and fiery flavour to this gourmet open sandwich. Roast the tomatoes on the grid or spade until they're pap, then cut them in half and rub them into the toast so that the juices and flesh of the tomato is absorbed into the bread. Then cover with a layer of salad leaves and onion slices. Place the sliced medallions on top of this, drizzle with olive oil and eat immediately.

YOU WILL NEED

2 ostrich fillets

olive oil

1 bottle of brandy

2 stale bruschetta

4 ultra ripe whole tomatoes

4 cloves of garlic

a handful of salad leaves, including peppery rocket

1 onion - *sliced*

1 clean spade

THE BEST STEAK RUB

1 teaspoon of:

- coarse sea salt
- brown sugar
- dried garlic flakes
- mustard and coriander seeds
- white, black and green peppercorns
- paprika
- bell peppers
- 1 or 2 juniper berries

Toss all the ingredients into a pestle and mortar and get bashing - what you are looking for is a fine granular rub to coat the hunk of meat.

This was one of the first meals I prepared for the Cooked crew. It's a really hearty dish and reminds me of all the things I love about South Africa. Waterblommetjies, simply translated, are little water flowers. They are indigenous to the Western Cape and grow wild in vleis and dams. They should be picked when at least half of the florescence is green, so when you see this, roll up or take off your rods. It'll be winter, so brace yourself, but if you're prepared to get your legs wet you'll catch yourself a real local treat.

WATERBLOMMETJIES

Lamb Knuckles and Waterblommetjie Potjie

★ ★ ★ ★ ★ THIS RECIPE SERVES ABOUT 6 ★ ★ ★ ★ ★

Make a good fire. Get your potjie nice and hot and add a good lashing of olive oil. Throw in the onions and garlic and let them sweat. Dust the lamb knuckles in seasoned flour, add to the potjie and brown the meat. Then add the stock, wine, tinned tomatoes, cumin, rosemary and the salt and pepper. Bring to the boil and then take away some of the coals – cast iron retains its heat well once it's hot – and simmer. Cook for about an hour and then add the butternut, broccoli and potatoes. When they are almost done, add the waterblommetjies and simmer until they are soft.

YOU NEED

olive oil

2 onions - *peeled and chopped*

2 cloves of garlic - *chopped*

1 kg lamb knuckles

seasoned flour

500 ml warm game
  or beef stock

splash of red wine

2 tins good quality tomatoes

a pinch of cumin

1 sprig of rosemary

salt and pepper to taste

1 medium-sized butternut
  - *grated*

1 head of broccoli
  - *cut into florets*

6 potatoes
  - *peeled, quartered and boiled*

about 600 g waterblommetjies
  - *or 2 x 400 g tins
  (if you can't find these guys
  use green beans, but they're
  a poor substitute)*

JAFFLES

Me Toastie Toastie Rise and Shine. Never leave home without a jaffle iron. Come to think of it, with electricity being what it is these days, don't stay home without one either. If you don't already have one, nick your mom's or look around second-hand shops. Then turn on the gas and go - you'll never look back.

This is the granddaddy of the snackwich and works on a gas stove, over coals or on an open fire. It's a really excellent way to use up leftovers and even not-so-fresh bread once heated through tastes like it's just come out of the oven.

If you don't have a clue what I'm talking about, let me explain . . . A jaffle iron looks like a long pair of tongs with identical convex circles of cast iron *(like earmuffs)* on each end. When pressed together these create a round pocket in which you place your jaffle.

Butter two slices of bread and place one slice, buttered side down, into one pocket. Then fill with a generous helping of whatever filling you've got before putting the second slice on top, buttered side up. Bring the two halves of the iron together and close tight. Trim the corners of the bread if the iron hasn't chopped them off already. Place on the stove or fire and cook for roughly 2 minutes on each side. This isn't an exact science, so keep your eye on the prize. The outer shell of a perfectly cooked jaffle will be golden brown and crispy and the inside hot and juicy - any cheese in the filling must have melted. If you're watching the waistline, Spray 'n Cook can be used instead of butter but, as they say in the classics, everything tastes better with real butter.

Suggestions for fillings

tinned chilli con carne

crunchy peanut butter, sliced banana, and honey
(you can use jam instead of honey, but honey is the tits!)

ham, tomato, and cheese

curried mince

bacon, eggs, cheese and tomato - *a great breakfast in the bush*

just about any leftovers work well - *so mix and match*

It's always good to have mates who live in strategically placed and beautiful spots and Swellendam is one of these - halfway between Cape Town and George. It's even better when, like my old friend Richard Walker, they can introduce you to local places where you can get your hands on knockout fresh produce. Bought pies are often nothing more than lumpy sauce and soggy pastry with very little meat - you feel fortunate if you get a piece of gristle stuck in your teeth! But there'll be no need for toothpicks when you make my roast chicken and wild mushroom pie.

ROAST CHICKEN AND WILD MUSHROOM PIE

Once you've made the effort to get hold of free-range chickens and other organic ingredients, the rest really is easy as pie.

FORAGING FOR THEMSELVES

All livestock, including chickens, should be allowed to live natural stress-free lives - to be able to roam around freely, scratch in the grit, roll in the mud and forage for much of their food. They should never spend their days cramped up in tiny kraals, sties or pens or be force-fed, whether they're being reared for the pot or not. We have to rely on reputable retailers to check up on living conditions and to market accordingly, but there are a few things that you should look for on the label. In addition to free-range, the product must be antibiotic and hormone-free and must not have been fed fishmeal or any animal by-product.

An added bonus with free-range chickens is that their eggs are much higher in the good omega 3 oil and they just look and taste so much better.

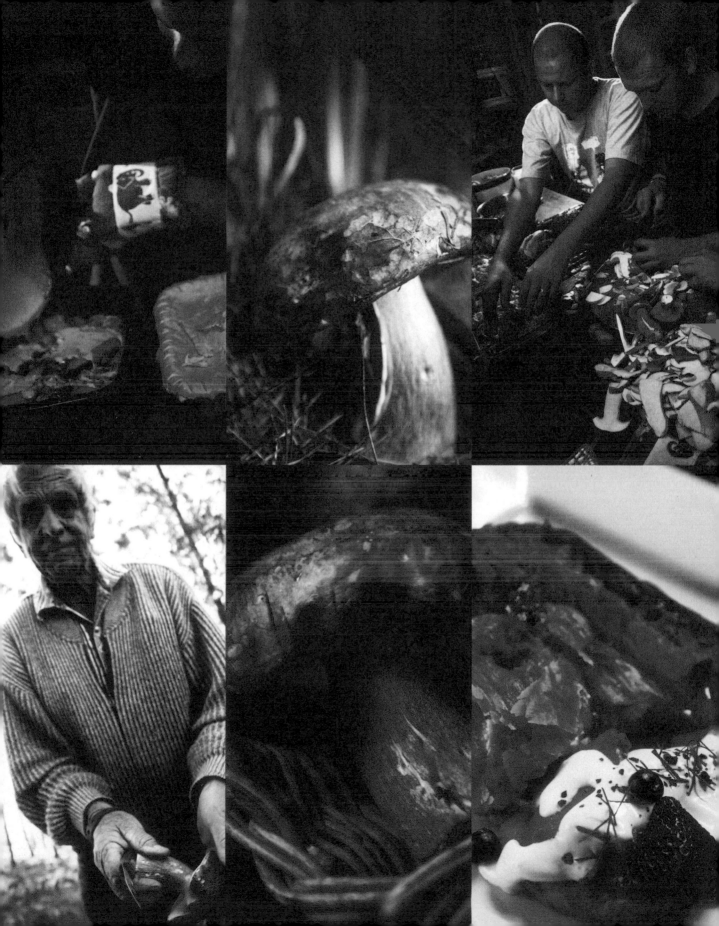

FORAGING FOR YOURSELF

OK, you have found the chicken, but before you roll up your sleeves and start baking, you need to take your partner for a little stroll in the forest to show off just how free-range you are. Although the wild mushroom is not exactly an aphrodisiac, it tends to make women more tender and men more likeable . . . reason enough to set off early before the hordes arrive.

Mushrooms are easiest to find on one of those drizzly, crisp winter mornings when you can smell the leaves and the mulchy soil. It's a case of the early bird getting the worm and don't forget to cut off the mushrooms just above the base so that another will grow in its place.

Porcini mushrooms (*Boletus edulis, Cep)* to me are the Rolls-Royce of edible shrooms. They have such an incredible flavour and once you know what you're looking for, they're easy to identify. But if you're as unlucky at finding wild mushrooms as I am at fishing, you'll find that good specialist food stores stock the dried product.

Or you could grow your own . . . The easiest way to do this is to let someone else do the basics and buy a mushroom growing kit. These are made from mushroom-friendly substrates like logs *(especially good for growing shiitakes)*, straw or wood chips into which they have injected 'spawn' that spreads and turns into mushrooms. You soak the kit in water and then keep it in a cool, moist place and literally watch your mushrooms grow.

Once it's up and running you'll be able to harvest a decent crop, and you can keep it going for years if you store it in the right conditions. Something like a plastic aquarium will do, or even wrap it up in a plastic bag - just make sure it stays cool and moist.

If you're lucky enough to land up with more than you can eat, dry the surplus. Build a drying unit.

Slice the mushrooms into about 5 mm thick medallions. Place on the drying racks in a single layer. Turn on the light bulb. More heat is generated at the lower levels, so every few hours swap the drying racks around. Repeat until the mushrooms are completely dehydrated, it should take about 24 hours - experimentation and practice make perfect!

You can also use your drying unit for other products, including thinly sliced apples, peaches, chillies and tomatoes. In fact, it's a great way to ensure that none of the bounty from your veggie patch goes to waste and that your pantry stays stocked throughout the year.

WARNING! MUSHROOMS CAN BE POISONOUS

If you've never been mushroom picking before, you need to know that the rule is never to touch wild toadstools or mushrooms unless an expert has checked them out and given you the green light. One mistake can lead to symptoms of sweating, cramps, diarrhoea, convulsions and liver damage and about 60 per cent of mistakes are fatal.

. . . can lead to confusion
You could land up having 'a-religious-experience-in-a-fungus'. The primary ingredient that causes this is psilocybin and a shroom trip can mean five hours of intense psychedelic colours and fluorescent light. At high doses all connection with reality is lost - monsters crawl out of the woodwork and mundane actions become hilarious. While tripping one should not handle anything more technically challenging than a plastic teaspoon.

. . . can save the world
Oyster mushrooms are becoming our great white knights, the grand recyclers of our planet and the trendsetters in habitat restoration. Industry is already using these pearls to convert polluted soil to a less contaminated state and some claim that they're capable of assisting in cleaning up toxic spills, halting poison-gas attacks and curing deadly diseases, and who knows what else . . .

NOW LET'S GET BACK TO THAT PIE . . .

Roasting the chickens. Rinse the chickens under cold water and gently pat dry. Rub them all over with olive oil, salt, pepper and thyme *(including the inside of the bird)*. Place both birds in your baking dish and roast at 180°C for 1 to 1½ hours until the chicken is tender and the juices run clear when it is poked with a skewer. If the juice is pink, the chicken needs to cook for a while longer.

Once the chicken is cooked, let it cool down, then debone it, breaking up all the meat into small pieces. If you're watching your weight, feed the skin to your dogs. If not, chop it up finely and add to the chicken pieces for extra flavour. Chuck all the bones and leftover bits into your compost bin or boil up for stock.

Rehydrate dried mushrooms. If you are using dried mushrooms, soak them in hot water. Do this at the same time as you put the chickens in the oven because the mushrooms need a good hour to rehydrate properly. Drain off excess liquid afterwards.

Pan fry the garlic, sliced onion and chillies in a small knob of butter until the onion turn translucent. Add the mushrooms and pan fry on low heat until there is no excess juice left, this takes a couple of minutes.

Make the roux. This is the fancy word for a white sauce made from thickened flour and butter combined with milk or stock. Melt butter in a pan, then remove the pan from the heat and stir in the cornflour - it will start to thicken almost immediately. Continue stirring for 1 to 2 minutes and then start adding the milk little by little. Using a whisk, mix it into the butter and flour mixture until you have a smooth roux. Once you've added all the milk, flavour with salt and pepper and a sprig or two of thyme. Return the pan to the heat and simmer very gently for 10 minutes, stirring continuously. If the sauce goes lumpy *(which it might on your first bash)*, strain it through a fine sieve or use a blender. When the sauce is ready, add the cooked mushroom mixture and stir. Then pour over your chicken pieces and mix well.

The ideal size for your pie dish is *25 cm long x 17 cm wide x 5 cm deep.* Wet the edge of your dish with a damp cloth then cut thin strips of pastry and line the outside edge with these to give the pie a nice double crust. Spoon the mixture into the pie dish. Place the 2 whole onions on top of the chicken mixture - this will prevent the pastry from collapsing. Place the rest of the sheet of pastry over the dish. Press the edges down firmly and then trim off the excess. Using the back of a fork press down the edge of your pie. Lastly, whisk the egg and give the pie an all-over layer of egg-wash using a basting brush. Bake at 220°C for 25 minutes until the pie is crispy and golden.

I serve the pie hot with a green salad made from whatever seasonal greens are available. I always try to include avocado and slices of granny smith apple. A salad dressing is not needed but a squeeze of lemon juice over the apple and avo will complement the flavours and also keep them from turning brown.

YOU NEED

2 free-range organic chickens

olive oil

2 teaspoons of Maldon sea salt

crushed black pepper to taste

a couple of sprigs of fresh thyme

Other ingredients for the pie:
2-3 cloves of garlic - *roughly chopped*

1 onion - *peeled and sliced*

2 chillies - *roughly chopped*

small knob of butter

300 g dried or 500 g fresh Porcini mushrooms - *cut into 5 mm slices*

2 whole onions - *peeled*

1 free-range egg

AND FOR THE ROUX

60 g butter

4 level tablespoons cornflour

600 ml milk

black pepper & salt to taste

AND ALSO

1 packet ready-made puff pastry, defrosted but still cool

THIS RECIPE FEEDS 10 - 12

By the way, a basic roux can be turned into any number of different sauces just by the addition of a key ingredient. For a pepper sauce, crush up some Madagascan peppercorns and add once the sauce is prepared. Other suggestions include various cheeses, leeks or spring onion, fresh herbs or cayenne pepper. I'm sure you can think of lots more - so go bedondered!

Never say no if the opportunity arises to help yourself to fresh organic veg straight from the earth. The smell of soil mixed with the pungent fresh garlic was mind-blowing on the day I visited a veggie patch in the Swellendam district to harvest this and some artichokes for the evening meal.

ARTICHOKES AND PASTA

HOW TO PREPARE THE ARTICHOKES

Cut off and discard the stalk and the bottom two rows of leaves. Soak artichokes upside down in heavily salted water for 30 minutes to dislodge any insects and dirt, then rinse and drain. Boil in freshly salted water for 30 minutes. Tear off the bottom leaf of the biggest artichoke, grip between your front teeth and pull while slurping. If it's tender and releases its juices, remove the artichokes from the water and let them cool in a colander.

Pull away the leaves from the stem and put them into a bowl to add to the pasta. When you reach the heart, be careful to remove the fibres of the white choke. Then stand the hearts upright in a baking dish and throw in some **cherry tomatoes, chillies, garlic butter, oreganum and brown mushrooms.** Sprinkle with **breadcrumbs and parmesan cheese** and bake in the oven until everything's cooked and the cheese is melted.

TO SERVE

Cook up some fresh tagliatelli and add the loose artichoke leaves. Then dish up the hearts and the pasta and tuck into a hearty, healthy meal.

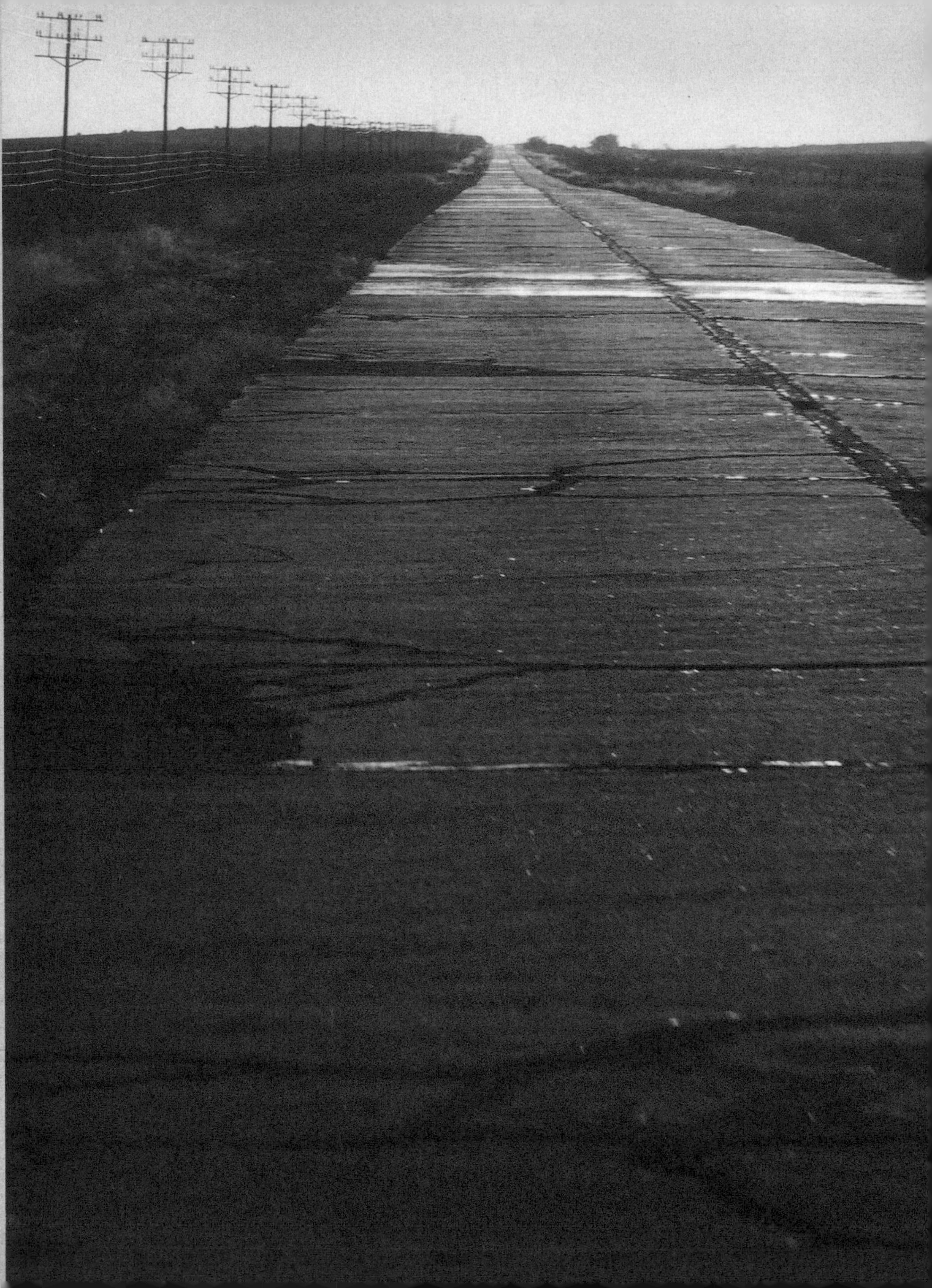

Heading down Route 62 and popping into every winery along the way would make this the 'lengthiest' wine route in the world. Being the upright Cooked crew, we wisely decided to steer clear and stick to the straight and narrow. Well, almost. We did stop off for the odd sip or two of supernaculum here and there - on the nail!

You'll find Calitzdorp right in the heart of Kannaland, just about halfway between Cape Town and Port Elizabeth. The Spa is a few kilometres out of town and is surrounded by ostriches, wild flowers and birds. Mother Nature has blessed its crisp clear Karoo waters with restorative powers that cure sprains, strains and even the odd kop seer, which makes it a fine spot to stop over and heal oneself.

CALITZDORP
0:1/0:2

2

BUTTERNUT AND SWEET POTATO RISOTTO

This is one of the very few times when I would say that too many cooks improve the broth, so ask a mate or two for help.

★★★★★ **THIS RECIPE SERVES 6 - 8** ★★★★★

Melt the butter in a pan over a low heat. Add a splash of olive oil to prevent the butter from burning. Add the onions and allow to sweat until translucent. Add the garlic and fry for 30 seconds. Add the risotto rice and stir until the grains are coated with the butter/olive oil. Add more butter if you like - this dish can never be too rich. Turn up the heat and add a ladle of stock. When it dries up, add some wine, stirring continuously. When the wine has been absorbed, add more stock, and continue this process of alternating between the wine and stock, and stirring continuously, until the rice is cooked. The rice should be al dente and creamy, with every grain separate. Season with salt and pepper to taste.

After you've added the third or so cup of stock, ask for some assistance with shaving pieces of butternut and sweet potato into the pot. The only way to know for sure when the risotto is ready is by tasting, so try a little. It should take roughly 30 minutes to cook.

Serve with a side dish of sweet potato and butternut crisps and a few slivers of ostrich carpaccio.

Carpaccio was first served in Harry's Bar in Venice in the 1950s. It's named after a Renaissance painter who used a lot of red in his art, because originally it consisted of wafer thin slices of mature raw beef which had been drizzled with a cold vinaigrette made from olive oil and lemon juice. Nowadays very thin slices of almost any tender cut of raw red meat and even firmer fish like tuna which is 'cured' in this way is called carpaccio.

INGREDIENTS

a big knob of butter

a splash of olive oil

1 onion - *chopped*

4 cloves of garlic
 - *peeled and chopped*

2 cups Arborio (risotto) rice

1 litre vegetable stock

1 cup white wine

salt and pepper to taste

1 small butternut - *peeled*

1 medium sweet potato
 - *peeled*

a handful of butternut and sweet potato crisps

a few slices of ostrich carpaccio

TOM YUM GOONG RISOTTO

(Hot and Sour Prawn Risotto)

Warning . . . this dish carries a ✱ ✱ ✱ ✱ *½ friend rating, which will keep your mates coming back for more.*

THIS IS HOW I MAKE IT

Grind, mash, mix and blend all the ingredients for the paste until you have a lekker thick, hot-as-hell sour paste or, if you've lost your sense of adventure, buy the Tom Yum Goong stock cubes from your local Thai supply shop and be done with it.

Spoon the paste or break 2 stock cubes into a pot and pour over 1½ litres of water. Add a punnet of finely sliced brown mushrooms - ideally, straw mushrooms if you can get your hands on them - a bruised stalk of lemon grass, 4 or so sliced spring onions, and 2 hot chopped chillies. Bring to the boil.

Throw the prawns into the pot and cook until just done, about 3 or 4 minutes. Remove the prawns and take out the stalk of lemon grass. Remove the stock from heat but keep it warm.

Toss the rice, butter and sesame oil into medium-sized pot and gently fry until all the grains are coated in the butter and oil. Then, while stirring, add the stock a ladle at a time, allowing the rice to absorb the liquid before adding the next ladle. Taste continuously until the rice is al dente - it'll have a glossy sheen to it and takes about half an hour. Add a final knob of butter and give it a good but gentle stir.

Sprinkle a few sprigs of fresh coriander and finely sliced spring onions over the dish, place prawns on top. Serve immediately.

Makrud Lime trees (*Citrus histrix*) are grown specifically for the leaves, which are used in Thai cuisine in particular. It is a thorny tree which makes it difficult to harvest the leaves, and they are quite pricey and not always easy to find.

PASTE

a handful of hot chillies
  - *I like to use bird's eye*

hand of ginger
  - *skinned and grated*

peeled stalk of lemon grass
  - *discard the hard outer leaves*

2 lime leaves

2 Makrud Lime leaves
  - *if you can't find these double up on the ordinary ones*

3 cloves of garlic
  - *peeled and chopped*

a tablespoon or two of palm oil

1 tablespoon fish sauce

1 tablespoon soy sauce

juice of 1 lime

1 teaspoon sugar

YOU'LL ALSO NEED

1 punnet of brown mushrooms

a bruised stalk of lemon grass

4 or so spring onions

2 hot chillies - *chopped*

18 decent-sized deveined and skinned prawns

2 cups of Risotto rice
  - *the best you can afford, quality does count here*

a large knob of butter

2 tablespoons sesame oil

This serves 4 to 6 guests, although in my experience they tend to turn a little piggish over this dish so maybe make a little more or invite fewer.

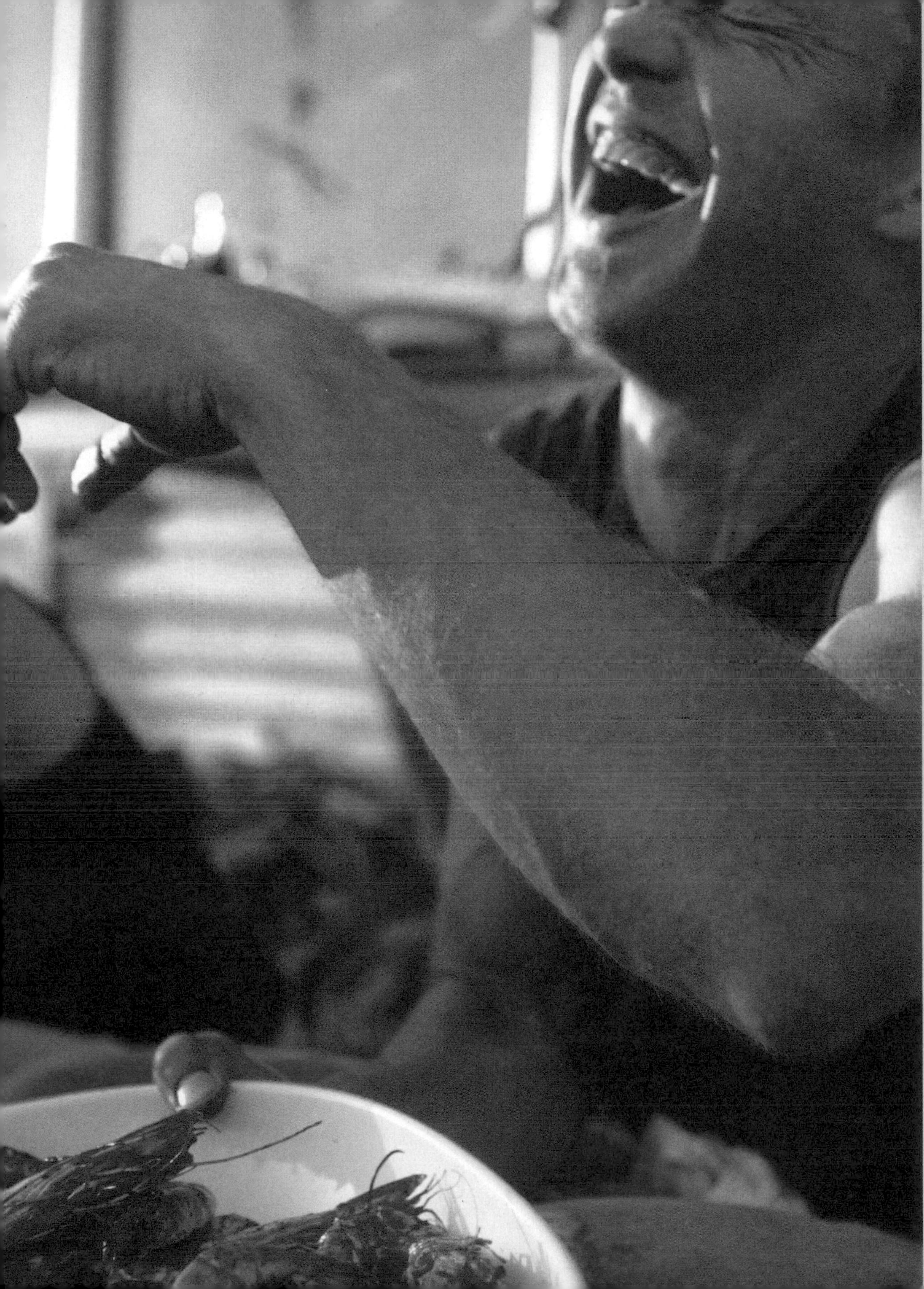

HOMEMADE ICE CREAM FOR THE KIDS

Rose Petal Ice Cream
(or any other flavour that might add a sparkle to your sweet tooth - think out the tub)

WHAT YOU'LL NEED FOR THE BASICS

1 litre full cream milk

1 litre cream

400g sugar

12 egg yolks

ROSE PETAL SYRUP

4 cups red rose petals

2 cups water

2 cups sugar

① Pour the milk and cream into a large pot and heat gently, stirring every now and then. Meanwhile whisk the sugar and the yolks in a bowl until they become thick and gooey and then add this to the milk and cream. Stir constantly. When the foam has disappeared and the liquid is the consistency of thin custard it's time to add your flavouring.

② The lekker thing about ice cream is that it's a base into which pretty much any flavour can be infused. Once you've added your flavouring, allow the mixture to stand until it reaches room temperature. If it isn't cool before going into the freezer the steam will form ice crystals. Keep your eye on the prize because you don't want it to get rock hard - give it the odd stir. When it's the consistency of soft-serve it's time to whip it out and serve it.

Rose Petal Syrup. Simmer all the ingredients for an hour over a medium heat, and then strain through a fine sieve. If there's any left over bottle and refrigerate, but remember to sterilise the container first *(see page 14)*.

MARSHMALLOW TREE // The Acacia erioloba or, as it is more commonly known, the CAMEL THORN TREE grows ear-shaped pods that are to heffalumps what honey is to Winnie-the-Pooh and as a consequence they'll pretty much go to any lengths to get their trunks on them.

We followed their lead - just added our own sweetmeat.

5

* * *

WILDSIDE

THE TIN CUP BREAKFAST

Hitch a lift from Knysna
Catch a wave in Buffalo Bay
Sit on the sand and absorb an
East Coast sunrise.

These are poached eggs - bundu style.

FOR TWO PEOPLE YOU'LL NEED

2 tin mugs
4 eggs

This basic breakfast allows for fillings of your choice - from mushrooms and crispy bacon to cherry tomatoes and mature cheddar and everything in between. Whatever combination gets you going! If it needs cooking (like bacon), make sure that you do that first.

Wipe the inside of the mugs with olive oil. Put in whatever ingredients you've chosen. Break two eggs over the top. Place the mugs in a pot with enough water so that the mugs are half submerged. Put the lid on and place it on the fire. Bring the water to the boil. This method of poaching eggs takes about four to five minutes, but keep checking. When the eggs are to your liking - eat them out of the mug with a spoon or fork. Ja, swaer, dis nou lekker.

I've always thought of hoboes as gentlemen of the road, and since I have been doing all this travelling I have an even greater respect for them. When we finally reached Buffalo Bay I saw the look in the eyes of a gnarled old vagabond as he hooked himself a cob. I just knew he'd wrap it in yesterday's news and cook it on some driftwood while he sat on the sand and watched the light on the water at sunset. Who needs wealth or a mansion when you're flying high as a kite in such glorious surroundings?

HOBO FISH

INGREDIENTS

1 whole fish - *scaled and gutted (Kabeljou works really well)*

salt and pepper to taste

2 tomatoes, sliced

4 cloves of garlic - *crushed*

1 onion - *sliced*

This is like the fish in banana leaves (see page 200), except that you use wet sheets of newsprint instead.

Score the fish with a sharp knife, cutting slits about 5 mm deep and 4 cm apart in the skin on both sides. Rub with salt and pepper and stuff the belly with the tomatoes, garlic and onion. Wrap it in about 10 sheets of newspaper, wetting each layer well with seawater before adding the next layer.

Chuck the whole parcel directly on to the coals of (*preferably*) a wood fire and cover with more coals. Leave for 20-25 minutes, depending on the size of the fish. When you take the parcel out of the fire, remove all the charred newspaper and place it on a fresh sheet. Then eat it with your hands - hobo style.

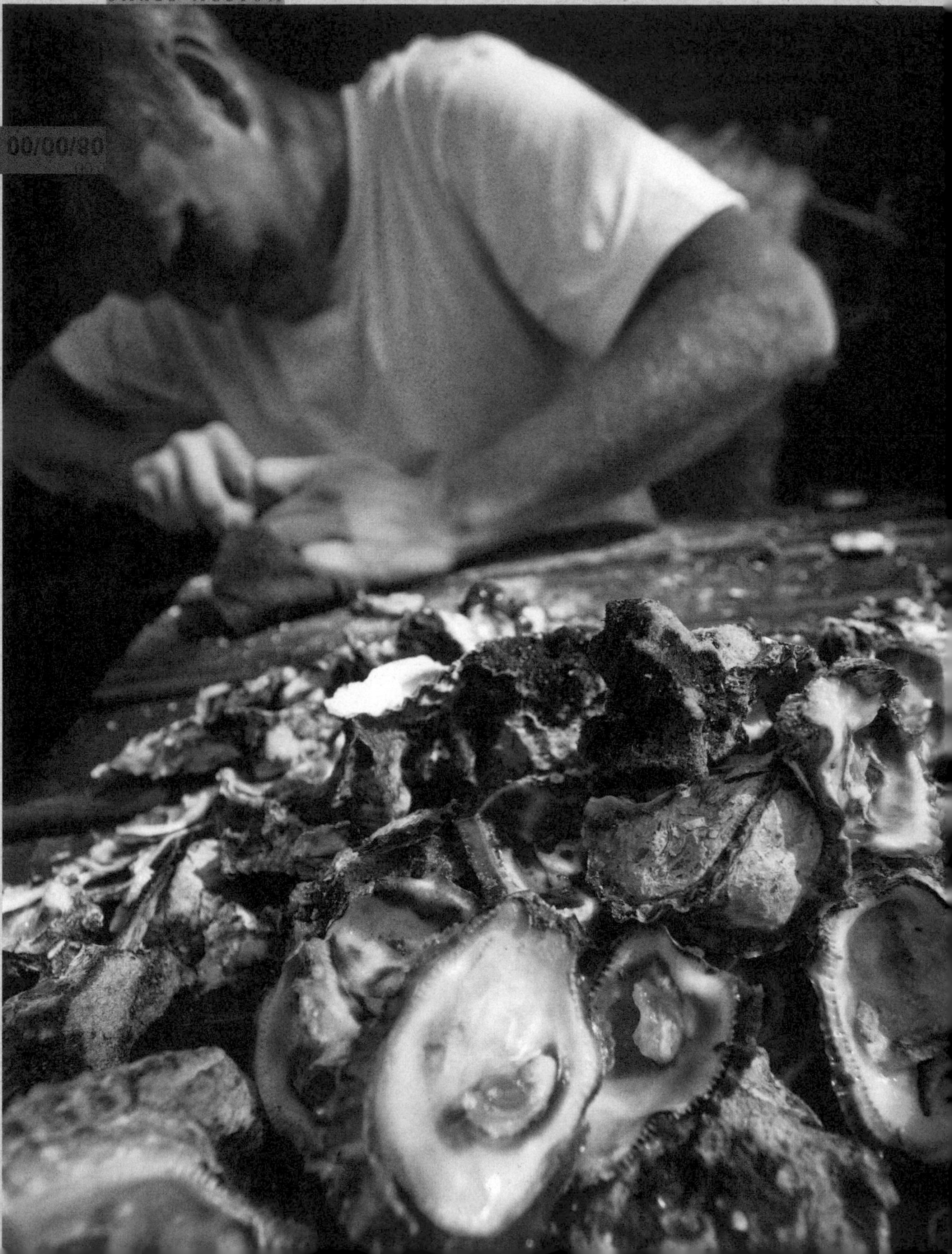

OYSTERS

THE SEDUCTION Fresh oysters are so alive, so naked, and so much more pert than a bunch of wilting roses. So creamy, so fleshy, and so much nuttier than any box of chocolates. Shucking . . . drizzling . . . lifting and rotating to find the smoothest spot to kiss . . . and then to slurp. Gentle nibbles . . . the release of subtle flavours and . . . the clean, smoky aftertaste.

Serve with bubbly or crisp dry white wine, or maybe even a good single malt. Casanova and his many mistresses would devour fifty raw oysters while sharing a bathtub designed for two. Why not fill yours with sparkling wine?

But before you plan this wanton meal, there's a reality check.

SHUCKING

First up, you've got to find a supply of fresh oysters. Most good suppliers will open your oysters for a small additional fee, and it is worth every cent. But if you've found a spot where you can harvest your own, be prepared for pain. Live oysters can inflict serious wounds before they release their physical delights. So don't think that you can use a screwdriver or any old kitchen knife to open these babies. If you're really going to do this yourself, invest in an oyster knife, sit down outside and listen carefully . . .

Wrap the oyster in a kitchen towel, and place it on a flat surface with the small indentation *(the hinge)* facing away from you. Insert the oyster knife into the hinge and twist back and forth. Pry the lid open wide enough to hold it up with your thumb. Try not to plunge the knife into the oyster - the idea is to keep it plump and whole. Slide the knife along the top half of the shell. What you're trying to do is slice the muscle that connects the two halves of the shell and lift off the top half. A couple of small fragments of shell might break off, scrape these away, then slide the oyster knife underneath the body of

the oyster and slice through the muscle that connects it to the bottom shell. Don't discard the oyster juice.

The first oyster opened is always for the guy who did it - slurp it au naturel. Now the bugger begins, you've got 2 dozen-odd to open, lad . . . but keep your eye on the prize.

From here on, things get pearlier. All the quantities given below are for 4 shucked oysters (except for the quiche, which requires 12). Mix and match or serve them all. Unless otherwise mentioned, always eat the oyster with its natural juices.

Advice // Seafood poisoning sucks! So make sure your oysters smell of the sea and not of fish. If you press the top shell and it doesn't close, discard it. If you're buying them go to a reputable supplier like the Knysna Oyster Co. Maybe you should order in advance to avoid disappointment.

① Straight Up

A splash of Tabasco sauce, a little black pepper and squeeze of lemon juice. *SLURP.*

② Oysters with Pesto and Gruyère Cheese

drizzle of pesto
small spinach leaves
Gruyère cheese - *grated*

Leave the oyster on the half shell, drizzle a bit of pesto on each oyster, then cover with a spinach leaf and sprinkle with cheese. Put on a baking tray and straight into the oven preheated to 250°C for approximately 4 minutes or until the cheese is melted. *SLURP.*

③ Tempura Oysters

1 egg
1 cup iced water or 1 cup
**   iced carbonated water**
1 cup all-purpose flour

Beat the egg in a bowl and add the water. Next, sieve the flour into the bowl and mix lightly. Be careful not to over-mix the batter. Dip oysters into the batter and deep fry immediately for about 20-30 seconds until the batter is golden and crispy. Serve hot with sweet chilli sauce.

④ Oyster Shooters

tomato juice
Worcestershire sauce
Tabasco sauce
vodka - *a good dash*
celery salt
freshly ground black pepper
lemon juice

Make a Bloody Mary by combining the tomato juice with the rest of the ingredients. Place two oysters in each 'shot' glass. Pour over chilled Bloody Mary. Mix. Shoot. *SLURP.*

⑤ Angels on Horseback

4 rashers streaky bacon
**   - *rind removed***
freshly ground black pepper
4 slices hot buttered
**   brown bread toast**
lemon wedges to garnish

Remove the oysters from their shells. Wrap each oyster in bacon *(it's quite difficult, but worth the effort).* Season with freshly ground black pepper. Place under a preheated hot grill and grill for 3 minutes on each side or until the bacon is crispy. Serve on toast garnished with lemon wedges.

⑥ Sexy Lady

2 lemon wedges
6 slices smoked salmon
**   - *cut into fine strips***
250ml crème fraiche
**   *(sour cream)***
a small bunch fresh chives
**   - *chopped for garnish***
red and black caviar
**   - *go ahead, be decadent***

Remove the oysters from their shells, drizzle with lemon juice and wrap individually in a sliver of smoked salmon. Place a good dollop of sour cream on the end of each roll and garnish with chives and red and black caviar. Serve on a bed of crushed ice.

⑦ Oyster Mornay

knob of butter
1 teaspoon cornflour
¼ cup milk or cream
½ teaspoon French mustard
2 tablespoons grated
**   tasty cheese**
extra grated cheese

First up, make a mornay sauce by melting the butter in a shallow pan. Take the pan off the heat, and slowly stir in the cornflour, the milk or cream, the mustard and the cheese. Return the pan to the heat, and stir continuously until the sauce thickens. Do not let it boil or it will curdle. Remove the oysters from their shells and put aside in a clean container. Rinse the shells thoroughly. Place a little sauce on each shell, place an oyster on the sauce and cover with more sauce. Sprinkle with grated cheese and place under grill until lightly browned. Serve at once.

⑧ Oysters Provençale

Cover each oyster with garlic butter and a thick layer of Gruyère cheese and fresh breadcrumbs. Place under a hot grill or bake in a hot oven for 5 minutes or until crisp and golden.

⑨ Thai-style Oysters

In a small bowl, mix finely shredded ginger, chilli and sliced spring onions. Add a tablespoon of lime or lemon juice, a tablespoon of sesame oil and a tablespoon of brown sugar. Mix all these ingredients together really well and put a dollop on each oyster.

⑩ Garlic Poached Oysters

In a small pan poach the oysters for 2-3 minutes in garlic butter. Serve hot on wholewheat bread.

⑪ Divorce Cocktail

Lastly, if you've got no plans with someone special, try this one. Shuck an oyster, slip it into a shot of tequila, give it a squeeze of lemon juice, a drop of the hottest chilli sauce you have *(I use Mozambican Devil Sauce or Bushman's Dynamite)* and throw it back. Then wait to see if anything interesting happens.

Cape St Francis is a fairly sedate and tranquil white-walled, thatch-roofed settlement with one striking exception - it's home to Bruce's Beauties, the world famous beach breaks that crash and bash the hell out of the shoreline, wake up the residents and keep the surfers on the edge of their boards. So we thought we'd dress in white to match the houses, serve calamari tubes in honour of the waves and for sundowners we'd knock back a couple of tequila sunrises and strawberry daiquiris, just to break the ice.

GRILLED CALAMARI TUBES
STUFFED WITH A TOMATO RISOTTO

We were lucky enough to get calamari that still had the heads, dangly bits and ink sacs, all of which we removed to use later. Then we prepared the risotto with which to stuff the tubes.

RISOTTO Make a basic risotto *(see page 109)*. Then blanch some whole tomatoes in boiling water and remove the skin before mashing up the flesh into the rice. When nicely al dente infuse with mussels and stoned, chopped green and black olives. Stir gently to let the flavours mingle.

Stuff the calamari tubes with the risotto and seal the cavity by threading a toothpick in and out. Now you have to work quickly, everything must be done and ready to eat chop-chop. Lightly fry the heads and dangly bits of the calamari in hot oil to which garlic, red wine and chilli flakes have been added, and then leave to drain.

Dip the filled tubes in oil, place on a hot braai for 30 seconds, turn and cook for a further 30 seconds. Remove from the heat and slice the tubes into medallions. Serve everything immediately with a healthy fresh green salad.

The calamari might be a bit chewy, but in most cases the methods used to create melt-in-the-mouth calamari removes all the flavour . . . and then what would be the point?

Everyone should try fly fishing. It's very therapeutic, even on days when you're not successful. Once you get a feel for it, the monotony of the ebb and flow of the water and the rhythm of the casting is really quite mesmerising. With a fly rod in my hand I can let my imagination run wild ... even pretend to be Brad Pitt in 'A River Runs Through It'. And it doesn't really matter if I catch anything or not because although it's supposed to be a fair contest I know the fish always has the upper hand. Seriously, though, it's worth mastering this ancient conflict between man and the denizens of the deep – or, more precisely, the beautiful trout and salmon that swim in tranquil rivers and dams – and the saltwater fish like harders/mullet – that swim just below the surface of the water.

Creating your own fly is quite a challenge too. They are made by tying hair, fur, feathers and other natural and synthetic materials on to a hook with thread so that it resembles the local insect that is attractive to your prey.

The fly is too light to be cast and it follows the heavier plastic coated line as it moves through the air, which means that unlike other types of fishing, fly-fishing is really all about casting the line not the bait.

This is how it's done. Hold the fly rod in your dominant hand and control the line with the other hand held close to the reel. Pull out small amounts of the line while you increase the backward and forward motion to generate more energy in the line. To do this properly the loops of line must extend completely in one direction before you throw your rod in the opposite direction. There should be a slight pause at the end in both directions to allow the entire line to extend parallel to the surface of the water. As your rhythm improves, longer and more accurate casts are achieved.

Don't be discouraged if you land up with tangled line piled up at your feet and your fly bobbing on the water ... it's happened to the best of us. As they say in the classics ... if at first you don't succeed, fly, fly and fly again!

ROOIBOS SMOKED TROUT RAVIOLI

WITH BURNT GARLIC AND TEQUILA SAUCE

'Country people are the ones who invite you into their hearts and homes and who blow you away with their kindness and generosity. Ja, the country people . . .'

They're great . . . and so is this recipe, the one that I made while my mates relaxed alongside a beautiful farm dam in the Hogsback district. Only fly in the ointment that day was my lack of luck with my fly in the water. Here, surrounded by mountains, forests, waterfalls and dams bursting with trout I felt a million miles from anywhere and it was easy to understand how this place was such an inspiration for J J R Tolkien's fictional Mirkwood Forest in The Lord of the Rings.

I'm not sure if it was the ancient Afro-montane trees or the overwhelming sense of stillness but I, too, felt the urge to produce, not a best-seller, but lunch for everyone. So at the crack of dawn I set out to bag me a trout. Our host's dam was the perfect setting and I felt confident, but the pressure of having promised to provide the key ingredient for our meal finally got to me and I think the trout must have sensed my anxiety. It never ceases to amaze me how these little devils, with a brain the size of a pea and a memory span of three seconds flat, manage to outsmart really skilled fishermen. But the locals lived up to their reputation for generosity, and one who'd been luckier **(or smarter)** than me was kind enough to sense my humiliation and come to my rescue.

So after building up an appetite on a gentle hike - not up the mountain, just through the forests to the waterfall - we settled down next to the dam to prepare my much-vaunted trout ravioli.

After the humbling experience with the rod I needed some Dutch courage. Thank goodness the recipe calls for a bottle of Agave Gold Tequila and a shot glass. I recommend that you klap a shot before starting - it certainly got me going!

For smoking the fish, you will need . . .

a smoking dish - *the bottom half of an ordinary deep roasting pan will do just fine*

tin foil - *enough to line the pan and cover to seal*

a fish grid or flat wire grid that fits into dish

. . . as well as . . .

1 deboned side of a medium-sized trout

4 rooibos teabags - *tea leaves removed from the bags*

1 tablespoon of honey - *that day I had some magnificent lemon and lime honey from the Tsitsikamma*

pinch or two of Maldon sea salt

For the filling . . .
Flake the smoked trout into a dish, add a fist-size piece of ricotta cheese and mash roughly.

For the sauce . . .

2 large knobs of butter

a head of garlic - *peeled and sliced roughly*

6 large tablespoons honey

1 tablespoon cayenne pepper

1 tablespoon paprika

3 shot glasses tequila

½ litre cream

matches - *preferably long ones*

1 good pinch of salt

For the ravioli

2 cups flour

2 eggs (*free-range or organic*)

Sprinkle rooibos leaves evenly over the bottom of the smoker or the foil-lined baking pan (*shiny side up*). Sprinkle salt and drizzle honey all over the fish. Place skin side down on smoking grid or wire/fish grid placed in pan. Close up or seal the baking pan with foil (*shiny side down*). Place over hot coals for between 7 and 13 minutes, depending on the thickness of the fish. Remove from the heat.

TIP: If you don't want to use rooibos tea, you can use any hardwood sawdust - think oak or apple wood, but not resinous wood (*like pine, bluegum etc.*). Most fishing shops and good supermarkets stock decent sawdust, and one bag will last absolutely ages as you only use about 2 tablespoons at a time.

THE SAUCE Offer everyone a shot of tequila then reward yourself for getting this far. Melt the butter in a non-stick heavy-based pan, add garlic and fry until crispy, but not burnt. Add honey, cayenne pepper and paprika and stir gently while increasing the heat to max. Then leaning away from pan, add tequila and light it using a long match. Burn off all alcohol (*the huge flame will eventually disappear*). Remove from the heat. Add the cream, put back on the stove and heat while stirring until the sauce is hot, but not boiling (*otherwise the cream will separate*).

MAKING THE RAVIOLI Place the flour on a clean flat surface and make a well in the middle. Break the eggs into the centre and using clean fingers, gently mix the egg into the flour. Once the egg has been absorbed knead the dough for about 10 minutes. Wrap it in cling wrap and refrigerate for about 20 minutes.

Sprinkle some flour on your work surface to prevent the dough from sticking. Using your hands, make small balls and put through the pasta machine on its thickest setting. This will give you a long, flat, broad piece of raw pasta, roughly 2 mm thick.

Cut these lengths into squares - 3 fingers x 3 fingers. Place small mounds of trout and riccota mixture in centre. Fold into triangles. Starting from the corner, and using your fingers, gently push pasta edges down easing out any air pockets. Pinch the edges with a fork to make sure that the ravioli doesn't explode into a soggy watery mess when you cook them, and put to one side.

COOK THE RAVIOLI. Bring a pot of water to boil, add salt and then gently drop ravioli into the boiling water. Cook until al dente (*roughly 3 to 5 minutes*). Drain and put straight into the pan of sauce.

*Serve immediately. **This is the only time that it's acceptable to spear your trout - as they float gently in the sauce.***

These quantities are enough for 4 to 6 friends, depending on whether they've climbed the mountain or just wandered in the forest.

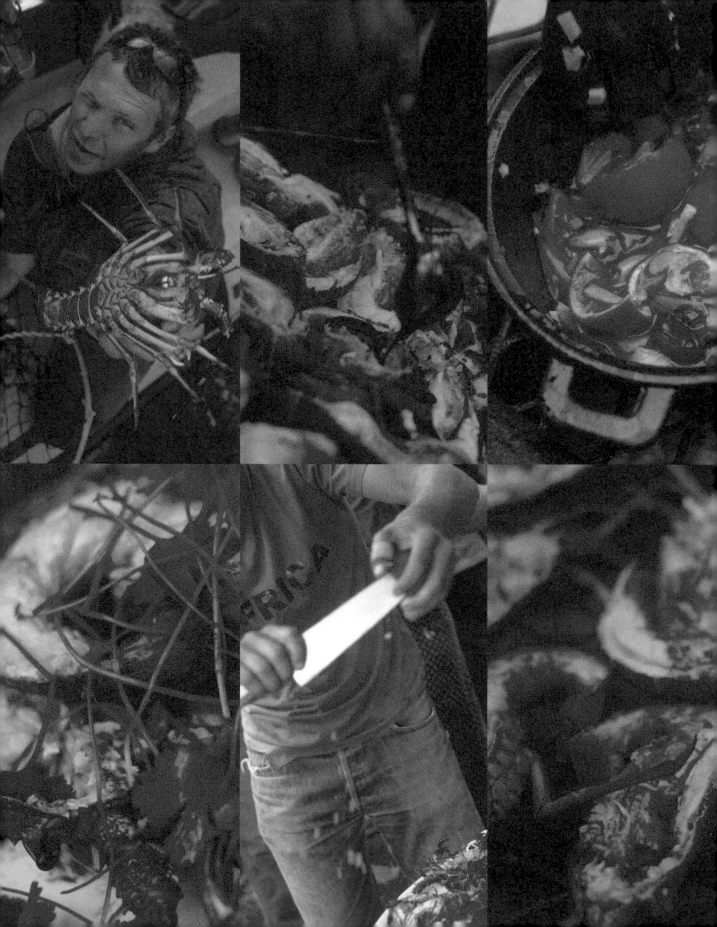

When gathering nature's bounty take only what you need because if you show a little respect nature will always look after you. We dived for these guys ourselves, something that isn't too difficult if you know what you're doing and stick to the rules. With Cape Rock Lobster, as they're officially called, there's the matter of a licence, the right season, minimum size and the maximum number that you can take out per person per day.

THREE KINDS OF KREEF: COOKED STYLE

① HOW TO CLEAN A CRAYFISH

Place the crayfish on its belly and insert a small sharp knife in the middle of the back where the head joins the body. This severs the main nerve and kills it instantly. Turn the crayfish on to its back and stretch out the tail. Using a heavy knife, cut through the middle of the shell from the tail through to the soft abdomen and the harder body shell between the legs right up to the head. Clean out the thin strip of the alimentary canal and pat dry.

② PREPARE THE CRAYFISH

Cut them in half - this gives you two lovely mirrored halves - and then steam them for 5 minutes - don't overcook them.

With this recipe the trick is to be prepared and have all the ingredients ready, so while waiting for your fire to be just right . . . **Make The Salad.**
Grab a selection of: fresh rocket, coriander leaves, baby spinach, mangetout, sprouts (*mung beans, alfalfa*), lentils, sugar snaps, sliced and seeded red, yellow and green peppers, baby marrows and sweet basil. If you can't get your hands on one or two of these substitute with anything you like. Toss all together on a large serving platter.

. . . and an angry but beautiful salad dressing
Go mad and chuck fresh garlic, grated ginger, chillies, peanut oil, low sodium soya sauce, sesame oil, sugar, sesame seeds and a good squeeze of lemon juice into the pestle and mortar and pound well. Toss into the salad just before you are about to serve the meal.

MAKE A SELECTION OF THREE SAUCES - CHOCOLATE, CHAMPAGNE AND THAI

① For a lovely chocolate-chilli and vodka sauce: Whack a knob of butter into a hot pan, followed by a slab of not less the 70% pure chocolate, three chopped bird's eye chillies and a generous splash of vodka. Stir well to allow the flavours to intermingle.

② For the Thai sauce: Chuck some butter into a hot pan. Add chopped fresh garlic and ginger and chillies to taste, as well as the juice of a couple of limes and a splash of both peanut and sesame oils. Stir until the flavours fuse.

③ For the Champagne sauce: Throw one finely chopped onion into a warm well-buttered pan, add half a glass of the best Sauvignon Blanc available and a flute-full of good local Cap Classique. Toss in a couple of bay leaves and allow to reduce over a medium heat. Drink what you've opened and socialise. Just before serving add 200 ml of cream.

Only start cooking when the flames have died down and all that's left is hot coals. Now when the coals are ready, throw the kreef on the braai for about 5 minutes, shell side down. Add whichever sauces you fancy and tuck in.

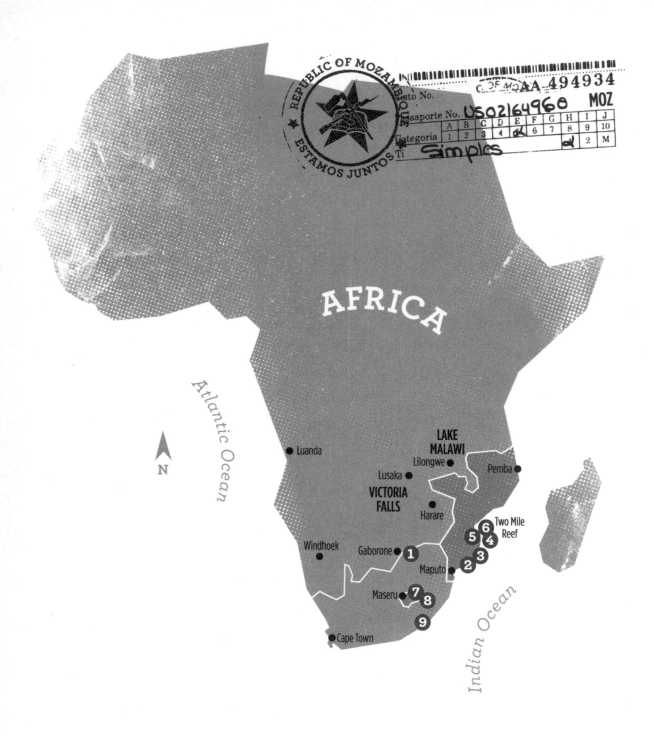

AFRICA

Atlantic Ocean

Indian Ocean

N

Luanda

LAKE
MALAWI

Lilongwe

Pemba

Lusaka

VICTORIA
FALLS

Harare

Two Mile
Reef

Windhoek

Gaborone

⑤ ⑥
⑥ ④

① ② ③

Maputo

Maseru

⑦
⑧

⑨

Cape Town

AFRICA CALLS

I've always had respect for a tree that produces useful fruit. The marula tree is part of the mango family and it grows wild in this northern part of southern Africa. The sweet, yellow fruit is used for jam - which is good - but it's also turned into home-made wine and beer, which the people who make it say is better. Then of course there's the commercially produced, lekker sweet Amarula liqueur that rocks on ice, and gives the skop to this recipe.

Is it any wonder that the local people believe that this fruit is sacred? They consume it to improve fertility and use it in a cleansing ritual before marriage but, most importantly, they warn visitors that to drink unfermented marula juice offends the spirits and is regarded as sacrilege. So to be on the safe side I'm sticking to the liqueur, even with breakfast.

There is no wiser beast than the elephant and for centuries there have been tales of how they 'gently warm their brains' by eating the somewhat overripe marula fruit. The fact that academics are now disputing this can only be attributed to their inability to appreciate the finer things in life. I only hope that the elephants take absolutely no notice of these ridiculous accusations and continue to revel in the effects of the fermented fruit. I know I will.

CRÈME BRÛLÉE

AMARULA AND CHOCOLATE

★ ★ ★ ★   **MAKES ABOUT 18 RAMEKINS**   ★ ★ ★ ★ ★

Preheat the oven to 150°C. Toss the cream and vanilla pod in a pot and heat through but remove from the heat before it boils and put to one side. In a large bowl, whisk together the egg yolks and sugar until the mixture is smooth. Then slowly blend in one cup of the warm cream vanilla mixture while whisking. Add this mixture it to the rest of the hot cream and whisk well - don't forget to remove the vanilla pod. Now here comes the tricky part. Divide the mixture between two separate bowls and mix the chocolate into the one and the Amarula liqueur in to the other. Enlist the services of a handy mate to help you fill the ramekins. You each take the same size ladle and from either side, simultaneously pour equal quantities of the two mixtures into the ramekins - and voila! A two-tone cup of custard!

Place the ramekins in a large pan filled with 3-6 cm of hot water and bake until set around the edges, but still soft in the centre, between 30 and 60 minutes. Take out of oven and leave in the water bath until cooled. Remove ramekins from water and chill for at least 2 hours.

When you're ready to serve, sprinkle about 2 teaspoons of sugar over each custard and, using a small blowtorch, heat the sugar until it caramelises. If you don't have a torch, place the ramekins underneath a very hot grill until the sugar melts and then re-chill the custards for a few minutes before serving. Very simple, very impressive and it's oh so smoooooth and just plain yummy!

PS. Use the egg whites to make meringues.

INGREDIENTS

2 cups cream

1 vanilla pod

8 egg yolks

1 cup white sugar

2 tots Amarula

3-4 tablespoons good quality dark chocolate, grated

extra sugar for the caramelised tops

Escaping from the pressures of the city does wonders for one's headspace and going to a place where time is neither 'money' nor 'of the essence' is better than any therapy. In Mozambique it's impossible to hurtle along a tarmac on which the hours are measured by a set of evenly spaced stripes - there are far too many potholes. Tomorrow will look after itself and a deadline is a big cat that didn't make it.

MOZAMBICAN MARKETS

As you trundle along the roads you'll come across traders offering anything from charcoal and wood to honey, furniture and even car parts - anything that they can forage from the bush and who knows where else. Business is done in a casual and relaxed manner, nothing is accurate, scales don't always weigh correctly, and everything is negotiable. The fresh produce markets are much the same, with the women transporting bags of goodies on their heads which they sell from colourful stalls. The produce is all locally caught or grown and is both organic and seasonal but you'll usually find fresh green cassava **(always cook before eating)**, lettuce, mint, parsley, coriander leaves, sweet potatoes, whole pumpkins, onions, garlic, chillies, tomatoes and cabbages. Sometimes they have oranges, lemons, bananas and papayas and exotics like green peanuts, cashews and coconuts - availability is completely dependent on Mother Nature. Fish is plentiful and crabs and prawns are readily available. Speaking Portuguese or having an interpreter is very useful,

and if you don't . . . watch your back and above all keep smiling and letting them know that you 'gostar' everything - being critical or miserable will cost. One isn't exactly spoilt for choice and the biggest daily challenge for me was to come up with bright ideas for meals using most of the same fresh ingredients. Imagine if everything in life was that demanding!

One learns very quickly that there's no point in getting hot under the collar and agitated about anything, including promises to deliver that aren't met timeously or at all. It's the good intention that counts and the locals are very forgiving of others who don't stick to commitments. They have a philosophical understanding of the many distractions, pitfalls and other interfering forces that emerge along the bumpy road of life and you would be well served to stay just as cool while you bask in the warmth of good humour - and explore the Mozambican way.

We were lucky enough to make this on a tropical beach in Mozambique, but it's equally lekker when made for mates on the braai in my back garden. We used kuta, or king mackerel, but any oily fish (like yellow tail) will do just as well.

CASHEW NUT BARBECUED
KING
MACKEREL

YOU NEED

1 x 500 g deboned fillet of king mackerel with the skin left on

2 handfuls of cashew nuts

100 ml olive oil

piri piri sauce
(blood hot chilli sauce)

4 ultra ripe tomatoes

2 stale bruschetta
(or pão if you're in Mozambique)

8 cloves of garlic - *peeled*

handful of salad leaves including peppery rocket

1 lemon cut into wedges

sea salt to taste

Make a paste by crushing the cashew nuts with a drizzle of olive oil and a splash of piri piri sauce - think of the consistency of peanut butter. Rub the whole fish fillet with olive oil and place skin side down on a cutting board. Use your hands to smear the paste all over the flesh side. Chuck the tomatoes on the braai to roast and sweeten. Place the whole fillet, skin side down on a grid and cook until the skin goes crisp and brown. As this was a hefty piece of fish, and was as thick as it was long, it was cooked for a further two to three minutes to ensure it was cooked right through. Cut the bruschetta in half and toast on the fire until really crispy, then rub the garlic cloves and pap tomatoes into the toasty bread so that they can be absorbed.

Lay down a layer of salad leaves on the bruschetta, place sliced rounds of the fish on top and add more leaves, drizzle with lemon juice and olive oil and eat immediately.

What a difference a day made! At the end of a long hot drive, during which we'd coped with the challenges of the roads, we arrived tired and late. The 4x4s had got stuck and I was racking my brain as to how to make the same fresh stuff I'd used the day before look and taste different. I started to feel that it was all quite hard work! Then the new day dawned and I looked out at the sea and I was going deep sea fishing and there were dolphins in the bay and the okes were catching and the water was magnificent and we were heading for a reef called 'the office'. It was then that I realised that this was exactly what a 'hectic day at the office' should be all about and I couldn't help smiling.

RISOTTO BALLS, SMOKED PRAWNS AND KUTA

A DAY IN THE SUN My dad always said that a day without wine was like a day without sunshine but we'd had plenty of both and I was a little sunburnt and more than a little hung over. We were out on a massive Hobie cat and I was going to prepare the lunch in the galley kitchen. But by the time we moored on a sandbank the tropical sun was just too inviting and I changed my mind about staying inside. So we spread ourselves out on the sand. But we stuck to the menu, which was . . .

SMOKED PRAWNS AND KUTA
Clean and fillet the king mackerel and devein the prawns by removing the black derm.
Cut off the heads to use in the stock, set aside a few pieces of fish to poach for the risotto. Smoke the prawns and then the kuta fillets using oak shavings *(see smoking, page 136)*

RISOTTO BALLS
Create a fish stock by frying up some onion and garlic in olive oil, then chuck in the prawn heads, a dash of white wine and whatever other bits and bobs you have. Everything *(literally)* helps with the flavour! Poach a few pieces of kuta in the stock until they are just cooked through, then remove and flake for later use. Allow your home-made stock to simmer, not boil.

Make a basic risotto *(see page 109)* using the fish stock, and when it's just cooked add the flaked fish and mix well. Shape into balls using a spoon, dip into beaten egg, then roll in sesame seeds. Refrigerate for 30 minutes. Deep fry until the seeds begin to turn brown. Place on paper towel to drain.

Serve hot with the smoked prawns, wedges of smoked kuta and a fresh green salad. Use your hands - it's finger-licking fantastic.

SALAD
Make a dressing of chopped garlic, ginger, grated cucumber and honey and drizzle this over a good mix of well-washed green leaves. Remember that if you use cassava leaves they must be cooked first.

We had aimed to be on the water at 7am sharp and to spend the morning leisurely paddling to the Isle of Pigs where we would be treated to a local-style lunch. But as a result of a colossal jol that had played out the night before, our group only staggered out of bed somewhere closer to 10. Finally we were on our way - our intended destination a rustic little island restaurant that specialised in local food. Set up as a community initiative, visitors kayak to the island and are treated to a slice of the true Mozambique experience, and in return the locals can earn much-needed income.

What's not often evident when watching our show is the lengths to which we go - in this instance, paddling like crazy in an attempt to catch up with the schedule. By the time we arrived the babbalas had really kicked in and all I could think of was a beer to quench my thirst.

But we were blown away by the massive welcome we received from the island's children and before we could say 'beer please' there was a soccer match on the go, using a home-made plastic ball. It escalated quickly, attracting both friends and crew. The pitch had no boundaries and roughly spanned the length of the island but the enthusiasm was infectious and headaches were quickly forgotten. Without a doubt the kids were the highlight of our visit.

I remember thinking at the time that lunch was a fairly humble affair of ripe tomato salad, freshly baked bread, rice and lovely local steamed crab. Am I kidding! You won't find fresh crab of this calibre on the menu of the hottest seafood restaurants in any major SA city. The lunch wasn't gourmet, but who wants that anyway? It was simply superb.

Bewaar op 'n veilige plek
Keep in a safe place

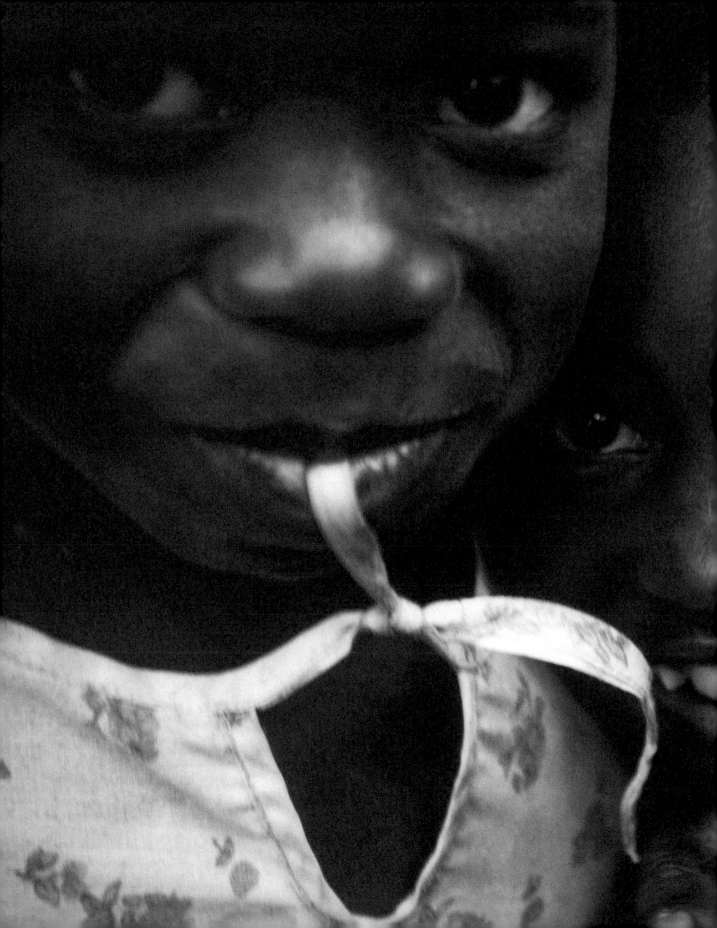

SPICY CHICKEN LIVERS

This is another little recipe where simplicity is truly key. Fry chopped onion and a couple of heads of garlic in a splash of olive oil, then add chicken livers. In the mean while make a fresh chilli relish with the following ingredients: **chillies** *(I like little potent buggers, but if you prefer larger sweeter ones go ahead and be boring!),* **coriander leaves, lemon juice, extra virgin olive oil and sea salt to taste.** Mung the ingredients together in your trusty pestle and mortar.

Once the chicken livers are cooked allow them to chill and then chop until they have a fine textured consistency. Now combine the chilli relish and the chopped livers and mix together thoroughly in a small shallow bowl. Pour melted butter over the top to preserve. Serve whenever, with toasted rounds of pão.

Note that I haven't given exact quantities here, as I find the best versions of the recipe are achieved when guided by personal taste preferences rather than instruction.

PS: You can add a splash of cream to give it a smooth rich texture but, hey, that's up to you.

The basic principle is that when wood burns, the smoke from the fire seals the meat and adds radical flavour. This process of preservation has been around for ever. When man discovered fire, he accidentally discovered smoke as well. I just like the flavour the smoke imparts and if you thought it was too complicated and way too much effort, think again.

SMOKING FISH

THE DIFFERENCE BETWEEN HOT AND COLD SMOKING

Hot smoking is quicker and takes anything from a matter of minutes to several hours. It's used for fish, meat or chicken and involves placing the food directly above the fire, or in an enclosure that is heated directly by the fire. The temperatures reached in hot smoking will kill any microbes in the food.

Cold smoking takes many hours, sometimes days, as the smoke passes by the food that is placed in an area separate from the fire. Generally the food remains at room temperatures during the smoking and no cooking takes place. So the inside texture of the food isn't affected and nor are any microbes present in the meat or fish. For this reason cold smoking has traditionally been combined with salt curing, particularly in foods like cheeses, bacon and cold-smoked fish like trout.

Firstly, hot smoking fish requires an oily or fatty fish, normally game fish - think snoek, think tuna, think shad, think harder or mullet. In my opinion, this is better because oily, fattier fish seem to stand up to the smoke, which adds lovely flavour. So head off to your fishmonger and ask him to scale and butterfly your choice. Very importantly, the skin must be left on as most of the flavour *(collagen)* in fish is in the skeleton and skin. So lose the skin to your own gastronomic detriment.

Next up, you have to dry the fish. There are two ways to do this. The first is quicker and easier but ultimately affects the flavour. Pat the fish dry with paper towel or, better, salt the fish with a couple of handfuls of salt - I like to use coarse Maldon sea salt

- and let it rest for 20-30 minutes *(depending on the size of the fish)*. Then rinse off all the salt under running water and dry the fish well using paper towel. Hang in a nice cool windy spot until the fish is tacky to the touch *(about 2-3 hours)*. Now the fillets are ready to smoke *(Follow the method given on page 136)*.

TO SERVE Take your fish out of the smoker. Place a couple of knobs of butter on the fish. Eat immediately with fresh bread, a green salad and a glass of your favourite white wine. If there are leftovers, or you overdo the fish *(and there is a good chance that you might)*, they can quickly be made into pâté and eaten on Melba toast within two days. This is a great alternative.

SMOKED FISH PÂTÉ

Smoke your fish, and then let it cool. Remove bones and skin. Flake the fish and combine with the rest of the ingredients using a fork. You could use a blender, but doing this by hand means you get a chunkier pâté. Season and serve with fresh bread or crackers.

250 g oily fish - *I used Kuta*

¼ cup cream

small knob of butter at room temperature

juice of 1 lemon

salt and pepper to taste

We travelled by boat, obviously, as that's the only way to experience the spectacular coastline from Vilanculos to Bazaruto Island, which is located at the tip of the Bazaruto Archipelago. As our feet hit dry sand we were welcomed with smiles, tropical flower necklaces and island-style cocktails - and this was just the beginning. This speck in the ocean definitely gets my vote for a perfect island getaway. It's exquisite for snorkelling and diving and, most importantly in my book, boasts some of the best game fishing in the world. This was one opportunity that I was not going to pass up.

As a consequence 'Cooked' changed to 'Hooked' for this episode. But once again all the talk of easy fishings jinxed my chances and, first up, the only thing I managed to lure was a little Boney, which is inedible. I was pumped, though, that at least it was caught on camera, which was obviously a sign that my luck was changing. The next day was make or break for me, so out to sea we went. This time the fish gods, maybe even Neptune himself, were on my side and I landed a Bone Fish, also on camera for all the world to witness, nogal! This has got to go down as one of the top five places we visited and for fishing it ranks Number One.

SUSHI
'COOKED'-STYLE

Creating sushi is just as much a craft as it is a culinary experience. While in Japan they believe that it takes as much as ten years to become proficient in this art form, if you follow my two simple rules you'll love what you produce. Truth is, if I were a purist I'd call mine sashimi not sushi - it's just one small portion in the sushi spectrum and it will take a little longer for you to master the entire palette. However, this is my creative contribution on how to serve beautiful fresh firm fish that's as pleasing to the eye as it is to the palate.

There're only a couple of rules when it comes to my brand of sushi. **The first**, and by far the most important, is that the fish you use is so fresh that it's still flapping. **The second** is that you use a razor-sharp knife to slice it ultra thin - about 3 mm slices of raw fish fillets - then arrange nicely and serve as is.

If you like, offer a good low-sodium soya sauce, wasabi (hot green Japanese horseradish) and gari (pickled ginger) as accompaniments - not that fish this fresh needs any flavour enhancers.

BÃO

is one of the many names used for any number of a vast variety of similar board games that have been played throughout Africa and South East Asia for at least 3000 years. The common feature is that the playing area or board consists of a number of pits arranged in two or four rows. In Mozambique we saw hundreds of differently carved bão boards but you can also play by digging holes in the ground or drawing circles on cardboard. The playing pieces can be Marula seeds or any other seed, bean, stone, nut or shell. The rules change from tribe to tribe and from place to place and vary from simple to very complicated but this is how we were taught and it's reasonably easy to grasp and great fun - so give it a go. The object of the game is to capture more seeds than your opponent does. Our board consists of two rows of six pits. Each player owns the six pits closest to him. And two bigger pits called stores, which are used for holding each player's captured seeds. You need 48 seeds. At the start of the game these are evenly distributed in the 12 pits - four seeds to a pit.

Rules
START

Toss a coin to see which player goes first. To make a move a player picks up all the seeds in any one of the pits in his row. Then moving anti-clockwise around the board, along his row to the opponent's and round again to his, he sows one seed at a time in each pit as he passes, until all the seeds in his hand are used up. If on any turn there are enough seeds in his hand so that he gets back to the pit at which he started then he must bypass that pit, leaving it empty, and continue sowing in the next pit until his hand is empty. Unless he is able to capture *(see below)* when his hand is empty his turn is finished and he 'sleeps'

NEXT PLAYER

The other player now has a turn and proceeds to move also anti-clockwise from his perspective, in the same manner as the first player, and so on.

CAPTURE

A player can capture seeds when during his turn, the last seed in his hand is sown in a pit on the opponent's side and the number of seeds in that pit, including the seed which the player has just sown, totals either two or three. Then the player 'eats' all the seeds in that pit, leaving it empty. If the pit just before this last one also holds either two or three seeds he eats these too and so he continues to eat all the seeds moving clockwise. He continues to move backwards, picking up the seeds until he reaches a pit belonging to his opponent that holds either less than two or more than three seeds or he gets back to one of his own pits.

SLEEP

When he reaches a pit belonging to the opponent which hold either less than two or more than three seeds or gets back to one of his own pits, his turn is finished and he places all the seeds that he has in his hand in his store pit.

FORCED MOVE

If any player, when he starts his turn, sees that the opponent has ended his move with no seeds in any of his own pits and the player can make a move that will leave seeds in one or more of the opponent's pits, then he must make that move.

GAME END

The game ends when a player, at the start of his turn, finds he has no seeds to move because all of his pits are empty.

SCORING

The player who still has seeds on the board adds these to his captured seeds, then each player adds up all the seeds in his store pit and the player with the most seeds is the winner.

STALEMATE

Sometimes there might just be a few remaining seeds in play on both sides but neither player is going to be able to capture any of the other side's seeds. Then the players agree to end the game and each player adds the seeds in his pits to the seeds in his store pit and the one with the most seeds is the winner.

5.00

LESOTHO

086 6632 2815 0 0040

16 6632 2 15

202

0 0040

This is just a tad refined and is a really cool way to do a mass breakfast for your friends on your next getaway. It needs an oven - but even a gas one can cook these rippers.

BREAKFAST
CUPS

Cut enough 10 cm x 10 cm squares of puff pastry to fill all the cups in the muffin tray. Line each cup with pastry and blind bake *(fancy term for partially bake)* in a fairly hot oven for about five to ten minutes - until they just start going brown. Then break an egg into each cup and bake until the egg just sets *(think soft-boiled)*. Now for the fun part - the toppings: if your tray has 12 cups make 4 of each variation.

① **smoked salmon and cream cheese with chives or spring onions**
② **grilled bacon and mushroom with grated Gruyère cheese**
③ **tomato and mushroom with fried onions**

Precook any ingredients that need to be well done *(like the bacon)*, then sprinkle, rip and tear the toppings over your soft baked eggs. Grill for three to four minutes. Serve hot with a twist of black pepper and a pinch of salt.

YOU'LL NEED
a 12 large-cup muffin tray
a roll of puff pastry
12 eggs

TOPPINGS
smoked salmon
cream cheese
chives or spring onions
bacon
sliced brown mushrooms
Gruyère cheese *(fondue cheese)*
sliced tomatoes
sliced onion

After an incredibly humbling visit to an authentic local home in the Lesotho Mountains, where we were treated to a deliciously simple snack of freshly baked mountain rolls, and I was able to look on and learn how it's done (see recipe, page 211), we hotfooted it down the Sani Pass to the Underberg. Splashy Fen music festival is held on a farm here in the southern Drakensberg every Easter weekend and we were ready to take in the music and cheer on the artists. This event has done a lot to shape authentic South African contemporary music and showcase our very own fusion of styles and cultures. It's been great at fostering a feeling of togetherness between previously diverse artists and, most of all, it's a really good jol. Although it was wet underfoot we stayed high and dry. But before setting off I prepared a little soul food to keep the band and crew rocking for the longest time.

DUSTBIN PIZZA

YOUR OWN PIZZA OVEN IN 15 MINUTES

Before you start, buy yourself a metal dustbin with a lid, or score a 45-gallon metal drum *(the kind that we used to halve and turn into braais)*. These old drums are becoming rare so go down to a scrapyard and have a look around, but first have a squiz because you just might have one gathering dust behind the shed in your own backyard. If you find one, wash it out thoroughly - in fact, give the inside a good scrubbing just to be sure. Also pop down to your local hardware store and pick up two unglazed quarry tiles made from red clay *(terracotta tiles)*. *Make sure they're unglazed or you could end up poisoning the masses.*

If you're doing this at home look for a quiet unused corner in your garden. Lay down the drum on its side and cover with soil. Clay has the best insulation properties of all soil and will keep your pizza oven piping hot, so if this is going to be a permanent fixture *(and, trust me, it will)*, try to get hold of some clay - otherwise use whatever soil you have. Place three bricks on either side of the drum to keep it from rolling and dislodging the soil.

THE BEST PIZZA DOUGH

500 g white bread flour
a big pinch of salt
10 g yeast
325 ml warm water

Combine the flour and the salt in a large mixing bowl. Activate and dissolve the yeast by placing it in a bowl and adding the warm water. *(The water must not be hotter than 45°C as this will kill the yeast.)* Give it a stir, and sprinkle a handful of flour over the mixture to prevent the yeast from forming a crust. Leave the yeast mixture for 10 minutes - it'll begin to froth - and then gradually add it to the flour, mixing it well until it forms a dough. The only way to do this is with your hands. If the dough is too sticky, add a bit more flour; if it's too dry, add a splash more water, and so on. Knead for 10 minutes until the dough has a smooth, elastic consistency. Sprinkle some flour on your work surface, place the dough on the flour and cover with a damp tea towel. Leave the dough to rise for 30 minutes - until it doubles in size. The damp tea towel will prevent it from drying out.

Sprinkle some flour on a clean work surface and then tear off a fist-sized piece of dough. Using your fingers or a rolling pin spread it into a circle about the same size as the clay tile. Make the dough as thin as you like - just be careful not to tear it. The border can be slightly thicker as it will give the pizza a lovely crispy edge when baked. Once you've perfected the base, let your imagination run wild. The numbers of pizza variations you can make really are endless.

READY FOR ACTION

Drain the tin of tomatoes. *(I use the liquid from the tinned tomatoes to make a killer Bloody Mary to sip while I'm doing the rest.)* Using your hands, mash the tomatoes into small chunks. Season with salt and pepper. Using the back of a spoon, spread the flavoured tomato evenly over the base - not too much or the pizza will become soggy. Drizzle with olive oil, sprinkle over some parmesan and garlic, rip up a couple of basil leaves, and finally top with pieces of mozzarella and some wafer-thin slices of pancetta.

Make a fire with real wood or charcoal in the back of the drum, never ever use briquettes as they give an awful flavour to anything that you cook with them, and what gives home-made pizza its authentic taste is the wood smoke in the oven. Don't go mad - it's an oven, not a furnace. Next, stack the two tiles horizontally towards the front of the oven and allow them to heat up. The tiles are essential because they ensure that when you bake your pizza, it's heated from the bottom and you end up with a crisp crunchy base. You may need to add another piece of wood every now and then to keep the heat up.

Place your pizza on the heated tiles and tilt the lid over the mouth of the bin to keep it insulated. Crack a cold one, and come back in six or seven minutes, or slightly longer if you prefer a crispier base. Remove and eat immediately.

HOT TIP *It's very important always to make sure you have oven gloves on a hot standby. The drum is made from steel, and obviously heats up, so always use gloves when going anywhere near the oven or moving the lid.*

If you are too slap gat to make your own oven, at least buy some unglazed terracotta tiles and try this in your normal oven. Preheat to 250°C and bake your pizza for 6-10 minutes. It won't have that lovely wood flavour but it still works pretty well.

MY FAVOURITE PIZZA TOPPING

tin of whole peeled tomatoes
  - preferably Italian
salt and fresh crushed pepper
olive oil *- use any one of the many great local olive oils around*
finely grated parmesan cheese
roughly chopped garlic
  (not the pre-crushed stuff)
fresh sweet basil
a block of mozzarella cheese
  - roughly sliced
home-made pancetta

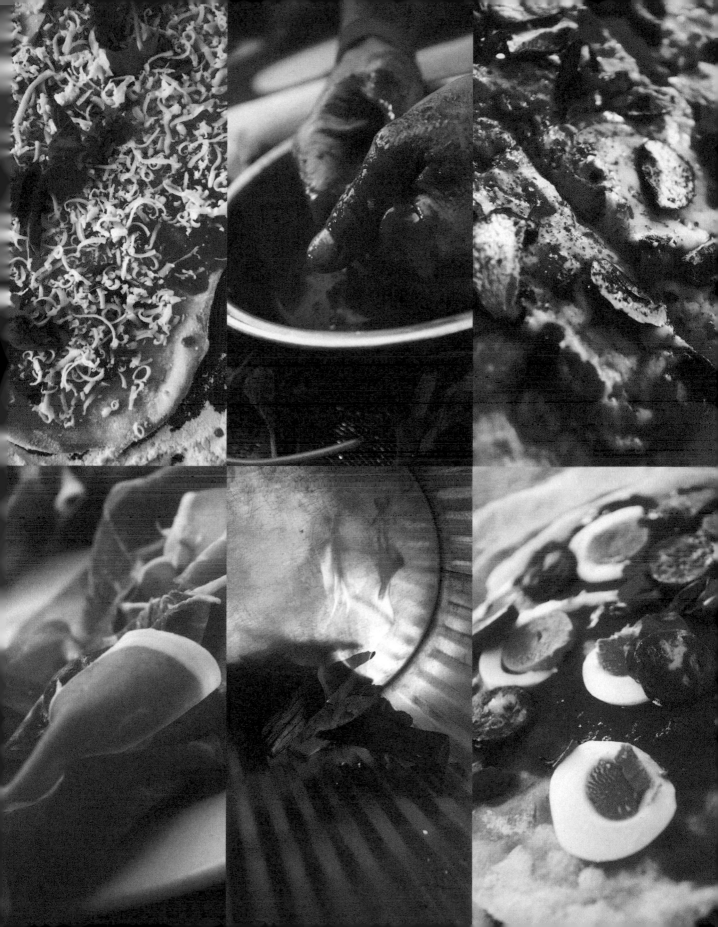

I first tried this on the Transkei Wild Coast with a group of friends who were spending a lazy day on a mile-long white beach backed by cliffs and surrounded by rolling green hills. One of the mates caught a Kabeljou and literally moments later it was scaled, gutted and filleted and one half was baking on the fire in what was available - a banana leaf. If you can't get banana leaves, you can use tinfoil, but only as a last resort. Try your best to find some leaves - you'll go bananas for them.

FISH BAKED IN BANANA LEAVES

YOU'LL NEED

2 kg white fish fillet with skin left on *(Kabeljou, Steenbras, Cape Salmon or Elf, also known as Shad)*

a handful of pitted black olives - *squashed*

a very small handful of capers

a couple of cloves of garlic

a small tub of cream

4 large banana leaves

a few pieces of wire to hold everything together

salt to taste

Lay the fillet on a banana leaf and place a couple of olives, capers and crushed garlic cloves on top of it. Pour over about 125 ml of cream. Fold the banana leaf over and tuck the edges underneath. Continue to wrap the fish in the banana leaves until you have a sealed parcel. Secure the banana leaves with wire. Place directly on the coals, or use a grid if you have one. Let it cook for about 10-15 minutes, turning the parcel only once. Don't worry if the outer banana leaves burn and turn black because the inner leaves and the cream will prevent the fish from burning.

Serve with some bubbly and a green salad while sitting on the sand and staring out across the water at the horizon. Sheer magic!

Just a little suggestion: Once you've made your stock or if you're on the beach and the gulls have finished picking, take the bones and guts and whatever else needs discarding, put it in a plastic bag and freeze it. You don't want this hanging around in the rubbish bin for too long because fish tends to go off very quickly. On the day the bin collectors come all you have to do is toss the bag in the bin, leaving your surroundings stench-free.

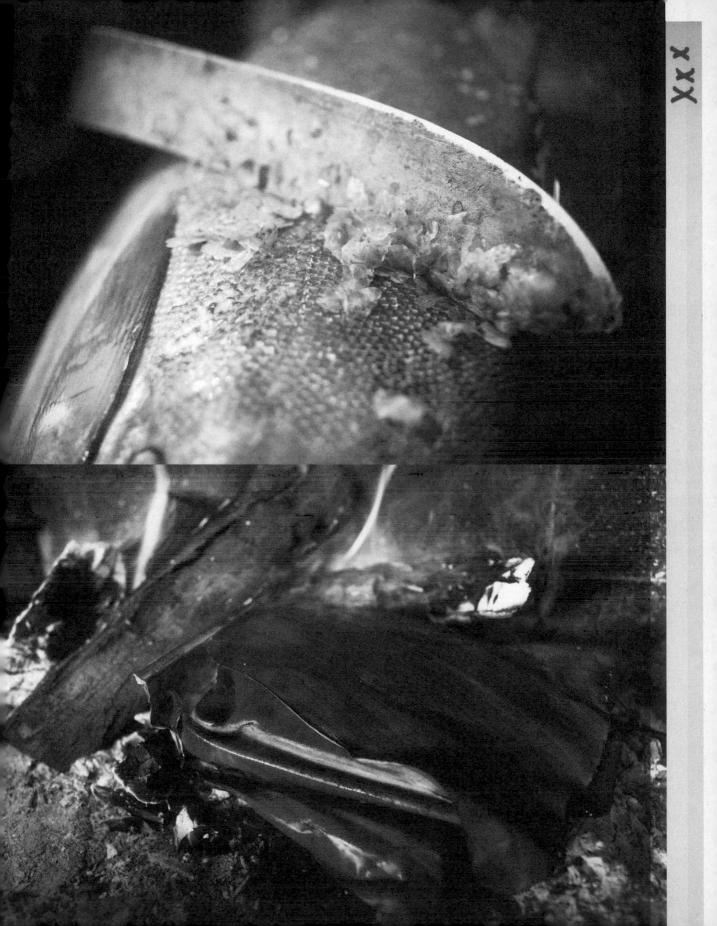

This awesome part of South Africa holds such a special place in my heart that it's almost sacred. The potent combination of natural beauty, simple bounty and indifference to the passage of time combine to create a wonderfully slow-paced culture and lifestyle. So before moving on we spent one last day diving, fishing and foraging in the rock pools. The sea was generous and gave us all that we needed - two blacktails, a bucket of mussels and sufficient oysters (including some slurped on the rocks) - more than enough to prepare one last splendid meal for everyone.

HOMEMADE TAGLIATELLI
WITH EVERYTHING THAT SWIMS

① I got the mates to help prepare the fresh tagliatelli after checking the settings on the pasta maker to produce the shape required *(see page 37 for how to make the pasta)*. Then I rounded up a couple of angels to spread out their arms and help it dry.

② Next, I cleaned and steamed the mussels *(see page 20 for cleaning and page 23 for steaming)* and made the tomato sauce *(see page 39)*, adding just enough strained stock from the mussels to give it the rich fresh flavour of the sea. I removed most of the mussels from their shells, but left some in their shells for 'decorative' purposes.

③ Then I filleted the blacktails, leaving the skin on, and shucked the oysters *(see page 125)*.

④ I pan fried the mussels and fish separately in a mixture of butter and olive oil and gently poached the flesh of the oysters so that they retained their shape.

⑤ Finally, I boiled the pasta, drained and dished it on to a large serving platter. I added all the cooked seafood to the hot sauce, gave it a few good stirs and then cast it over the pasta.

⑥ I gathered the masses around the table and we sat down to a last supper and a toast to this special piece of paradise.

XXX

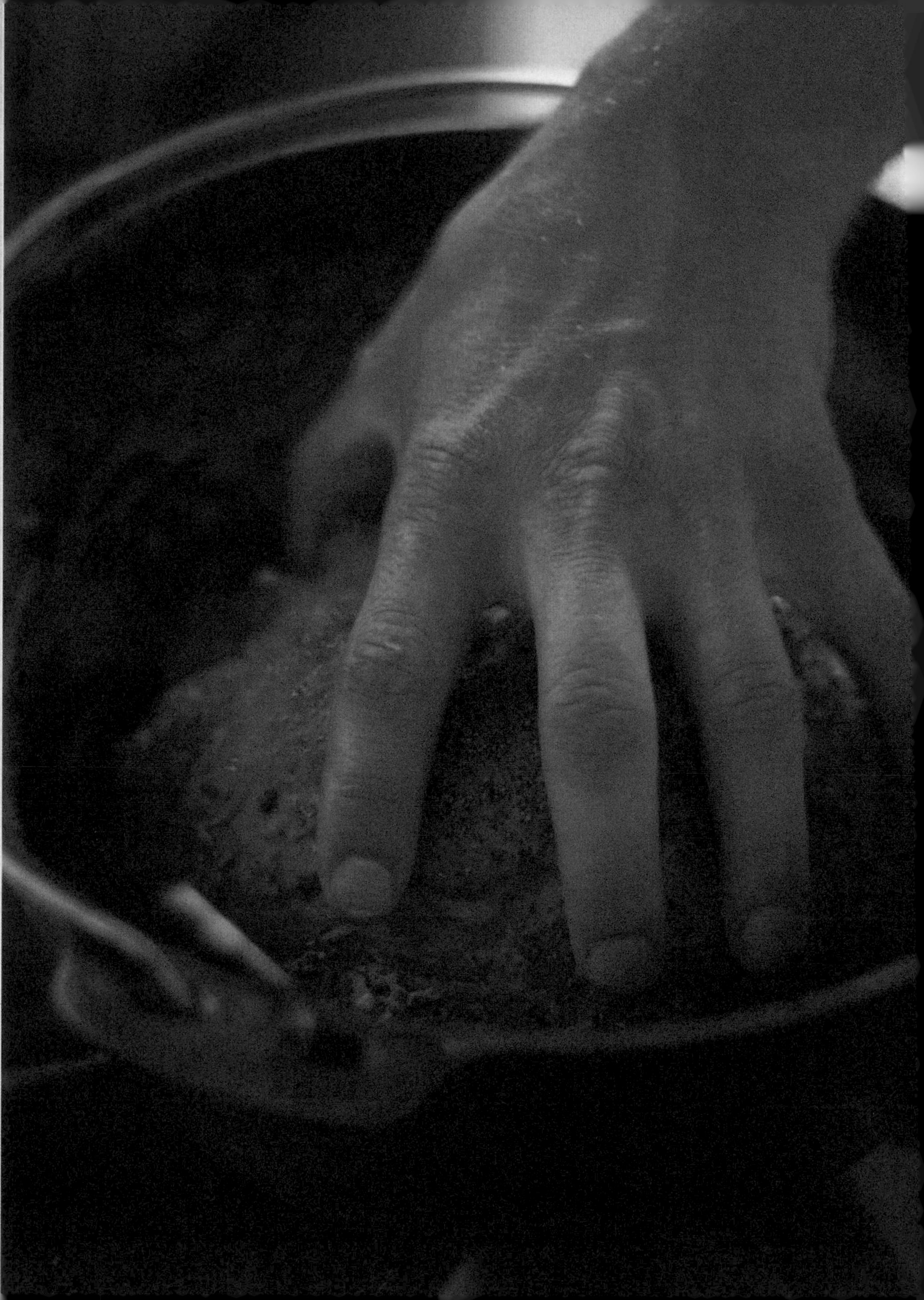

With fresh, crisp, steaming bread on the table you'll never go hungry. First thing, though, is to know how to make a basic bread dough.

POTJIE BREAD

First activate the yeast. Mix the sugar, yeast and warm water together, then sprinkle a tablespoon of flour on top *(this prevents the yeast mixture from getting a dry crust)* and leave in a warm spot for 10 minutes or until frothy. Sieve the flour into a bowl, add the salt and then, using clean fingertips, rub in the butter.

Next, beat the eggs lightly with a fork and add to the yeast mixture. Make an indentation in the flour, pour in the yeast and egg mixture and knead it well until you have soft, pliable dough. Brush the dough with sunflower oil, place in big bowl, cover in cling wrap or a damp tea towel, and let it rise in a warm spot for about 40 minutes, or until it has doubled in size. Knead the dough one more time *(this step is called knocking it down)*, and then you're ready - bake for 40 minutes in a medium-warm potjie pot - place a few embers on top of the pot to create an all-round oven effect.

BASIC BREAD DOUGH

10 ml dried yeast

4 ml sugar

100 ml lukewarm water

400 g flour

4 ml salt

60 g butter

2 eggs

sunflower oil

BEER BREAD

The great thing about this bread is that you don't need to knead it for hours and you can add anything from fresh herbs to sun-dried tomatoes or olives and fresh chillies to spice it up. This recipe makes one small dense loaf, or five medium-sized rolls, so adjust to fit the size of your pot and the number of friends for whom you're cooking.

INGREDIENTS

500 g self-rising flour

340 ml Savannah cider
or a dumpie of Windhoek

5 ml salt

15 ml olive oil

Put the flour into a mixing bowl. Make a well in the centre, and pour about two-thirds of the cider into the well. Start mixing. Add just enough cider to ensure that the dough isn't too sticky or too dry - knock back what's left of the cider. Cover dough with cling wrap, put in a warm place and leave to rise for 20 minutes. The trick here is not to overwork the dough.

This bread is cooked in exactly the same way as the Lesotho Mountain Rolls *(see next page)*, except that you shape the risen dough into a round wheel and place it inside the pot without rubbing with oil. The bread also takes about 40 minutes to become crispy and brown and ready to devour.

LESOTHO MOUNTAIN ROLLS

Make the dough using the recipe for Potjie Bread *(page 207)*. Rest your flat-bottomed potjie pot on three half bricks and push enough hot coals underneath the pot to create a low to medium heat - not a raging inferno.

Pour five tablespoons of sunflower oil into the pot to heat up. Break the dough into fist-size balls, dip them into the pot and rub all over with oil - don't burn your hands! Place dough balls around the edge of the potjie *(not lumped in the centre)*. Put the lid on, cover the lid with coals and walk away for about 40 minutes, remembering to add new coals underneath every now and then.

On your return, blow the ash off the lid, and open. Your rolls should be crispy and brown.

BASIC BREAD DOUGH

10 ml dried yeast

4 ml sugar

100 ml lukewarm water

400 g flour

4 ml salt

60 g butter

2 eggs

sunflower oil

This is a traditional recipe for bread made on a fire in the great outdoors or even in your own backyard. Doing it in the kitchen should not be an option but, okay, if you absolutely have to, then use the oven grill, but roosterkoek made on a fire just tastes so much better.

ROOSTERKOEK

First up, you have to activate the yeast. You do this by mixing the sugar, yeast and warm water together, then sprinkle a tablespoon of flour on top to prevent the mixture from getting a dry crust. Leave in a warm spot for 10 minutes or until frothy. Sieve the flour into a bowl, add the salt and then, using your fingertips, rub in the butter. Next, beat the eggs lightly with a fork and add to the yeast mixture. Make a hollow in the dough, pour in the yeast and egg mix and knead well until you have soft, pliable dough. Brush the dough with sunflower oil, place in big bowl, cover in cling wrap or a damp tea towel, and let it rise in a warm spot until it has doubled in size - about 40 minutes. Then knead the dough one last time.

Now comes the fun part. Break off a fist-sized ball of dough and flatten it with the palm of your hand. Put a good dollop of strawberry jam or chocolate or whatever you like in the centre and fold over. Press the edges down firmly and leave for about 15 minutes in a warm spot until it's risen to about double in size again. Then bake on a grid over medium heat coals until the roosterkoek is brown on both sides and cooked through.

If you're sitting round the campfire, wrap the dough around a stick and cook over the coals. When it's ready, remove the stick and fill the hole with strawberry jam and butter. You won't have to be told to lick your lips.

Moerse lekker with moer (ground) koffie.

INGREDIENTS

a pinch of sugar

10 ml dried yeast

100 ml lukewarm water

400 g flour

a pinch of salt

a knob of butter

2 eggs

sunflower oil

STRAWBERRY JAM

Making jam is really simple, just remember to sterilise the jars and refrigerate after opening. (See page 14)

YOU'LL NEED

1 kg strawberries - *cleaned and halved*
750 g sugar
juice of 1 lemon

Layer the strawberries and sugar in a container and leave overnight. The next day, place in a pot and heat very slowly, stirring occasionally to ensure that all the sugar dissolves. Add the lemon juice and slowly bring to the boil, stirring regularly. It takes a long time for the jam to reach setting point. Dip a jam thermometer in warm water, then insert it into the jam. When the temperature reaches 105°C the jam has reached setting point and it should be bottled immediately in warm sterilised jars.

Tip: No thermometer? Don't despair, there's always plan B - the cold saucer test. Put a saucer in the fridge for a minute or two then dollop a teaspoon of jam on to it. Let it cool for a minute then push the surface of the jam with your finger. If it wrinkles, the jam has reached setting point.

This was made on our way back from Mozambique. We'd spent five days travelling down from Bazaruto Island to the Wild Coast and we'd had enough of crab curry and other fishy comestibles. We were craving some solid boerekos and this was just the ticket. Think of a loaf of bread that's exploding with all the goodies you love in an omelette.

BREAKFAST BOMB

You'll Need 1 Well Oiled Flat-Bottomed №·③ Potjie Pot

① First you have to make the dough. Put the yeast in a bowl, add the sugar and lukewarm water - if the water's too hot, it'll kill the yeast. Sprinkle some flour over the mixture and leave in a warm spot for about 10 minutes or until the yeast begins to froth. Then add the eggs to the mixture and give it a quick twirl. Next, make a well in the centre of the flour, add the salt and the yeast-and-egg mixture and knead until you have a smooth pliable dough. Cover with a damp cloth and leave in a cool spot while you get your filling together. *Take note that unlike most bread recipes, you don't want the bread to rise too much. This is because when you bake it, the bread will rise so high that it will squeeze your filling out of its case.*

② Working quickly now, fry each of the filling ingredients separately *(except the eggs, baby tomatoes and cheese).* When they've all cooled down, crack the eggs into a bowl, whisk and add the rest of the ingredients including the cheese and tomatoes.

③ Roll out the dough into a big circle - think of a big pizza base - and place it in your well-oiled potjie pot so that the edges hang over the sides of the pot. Pour in your filling; this shouldn't be more than about 4 cm deep *(otherwise it takes ages to cook)* and then carefully fold over the bread dough and pinch the top closed. Put the lid on the potjie pot and bake on a fire by putting a couple of coals under the pot and a few on the lid. This needs to cook at medium heat. Too many coals will result in burnt bread, too few and you'll have undercooked egg.

As the coals die down, replace with hot ones. After about one hour open the pot - the bread dough should be crisp and brown. Stab the breakfast bomb with a skewer - if it comes out runny the egg hasn't set yet and the bomb needs to cook a little longer. If it comes out dry, it's ready to eat. Break off pieces and smear with chutney.

INGREDIENTS

for the bread dough
10 ml yeast

4 ml sugar

100 ml lukewarm water

2 free-range eggs

400 g flour

a pinch of salt

60 g butter

for the filling
6 eggs

1 punnet baby tomatoes

a handful of grated cheese

a handful of mushrooms
 - sliced

2 cloves of garlic
 - sliced and chopped

2 pork sausages
 - cooked and sliced

10 rashers of bacon
 - grilled on the coals

1 onion, medium size
 - sliced and fried

salt and pepper to taste

whatever else your heart
  can stand

Tip: Any left over dough can be made into fist-sized balls and cooked on a grid over medium coals for perfectly fresh rolls.

INHAMBANE

No. 743

BAZARUTO

VILANCULOS

ČALITZDORP
0;1/0;2

CEDERBERG

TREETOPS

HOGSBACK
01/09

FISH RIVER
CANYON
2.6 2.6

SPLASHY
FEN ★ ★ ★

GUGULETHU
'jija-letwa'

TOFO

3.6

MADIKWE
JAN
★ 23

CAPE COLUMBINE

WILDSIDE
08 0803

ISLE OF PIGS

Everyone has a story about Long Street where secrets are seldom sacrosanct. Mine emanates from a seedy pub in which I spent many a cold winter evening playing backgammon with mates. When my game needed upping I'd call for another little drop of heaven - a chocolate vodka. For some time the mystery of how to concoct this remained with the barman but my trusty palate and I finally figured it out.

CHOCOLATE VODKA

One massive warning: the combination of alcohol and sugar will rush straight to your brain, so please steer clear of operating any heavy machinery afterwards and of course never get behind the steering wheel ... And don't let on to anyone how to make it. This is our little secret.

YOU'LL NEED

one third of a bottle of vodka

2 slabs of your favourite plain chocolate

Break the chocolate into pieces small enough to fit down the neck of the bottle and watch them sink into the clear liquid. Put the lid on and immerse the bottle in a pot of warm water for about 10 minutes. As the water heats the vodka it gently melts the chocolate and the two become infused. Put the lid on the bottle and shake until the vodka and chocolate are well and truly mixed. *(You may have to return the bottle to the hot water.)* What you end up with is a sweet-chocolatey-goodness that's positively lethal. Serve as a shooter or pour over ice cream. If you're really feeling playful, substitute the chocolate with other sweeties - anything from smarties to jelly-babies. But if you are using chocolate keep it straight *i.e. no wafers, nuts or nougat - or it just becomes a soggy mess.*

KAROO OYSTERS

These barnyard jewels are not for the faint hearted. Cowboy caviar, lamb fries - call them whatever you like, but don't shy away until you've at least given them a try.

First up blanch the testicles whole in boiling water for a couple of minutes and then immediately rinse under cold water. With a very sharp knife, split the tough skin-like muscle that surrounds each 'oyster' and remove the skin. Cover in salt water and soak for at least an hour. Drain and transfer to a large pot and add enough water so that they float. Add a generous tablespoon of vinegar and then parboil, drain and rinse. Allow to cool and slice into thick ovals. Sprinkle salt and pepper on both sides.

Mix flour, cornmeal and garlic powder to taste in a bowl. Roll each slice in the dry mixture then dip into milk. Dip in the dry mixture then quickly dip into the wine. You can repeat the procedure if a thicker crust is desired.

Add a dash of Louisiana Hot Sauce to heated oil and fry 'oysters' until golden brown and tender. Remove with a slotted spoon or wire strainer. *(Don't cook for too long or they will become tough.)*

Drain on paper towel and serve. They taste exactly like really rich pork sausages.

INGREDIENTS

1 kg of fresh sheep, buffalo, boar or bull testicles

1 tablespoon vinegar

salt

black pepper

1 cup flour

¼ cup cornmeal

garlic powder

milk

1 cup of red wine

Louisiana Hot Sauce
or any devilish condiment in your possession

cooking oil

Justin's essential 'usetensils'

A BASKET - for mushroom and veggie picking - pick one up from the Society for the Blind

BASIC HIKING KNIFE, FORK, AND SPOON - I'll admit, sometimes bare hands just won't do

BASTING BRUSH - unused paintbrush works fine

BOTTLE OPENERS - have one in every room and bag; sometimes belt buckles just don't work

BOTTLE CLOSERS - one for champagne, one for wine and a pourer

BLOW TORCH - great for brûlées, crisping skin and roasting veg

BREAD KNIFE - for toast and sandwiches

BUSH TOASTER - you can use this on a fire or gas

CAN OPENER - chipped too many teeth; absolutely essential

CORKSCREW - have one in every room and bag; we've all been there trying to shove the cork into the bottle

GRANDMA'S MANUAL LEMON JUICER - manual is quicker

GRANDMA'S MANUAL MINCER - otherwise get one from catering suppliers

GRATER - get a small one for parmesan and de-rinding and a big one for the rest

HOOPED METAL HAIR PIN - best tool for extracting marrow from leg bones

JAFFLE IRON - snackwich machine for the fire

JAM THERMOMETER - for when you're preserving the fruits of your labour

LETTUCE DRYER - dry leaves make crisp salads

MEASURING CUPS - for baking (that's the only time you ever need follow the directions to the tee)

MEAT FORK - great for carving

MEAT THERMOMETER - to make sure you don't overdo your meat

MELON BALLER - presentation is important

METAL SKEWERS - as much as I like dangling marshmallows from a stick over a fire, sometimes it makes a lot more sense to have things that just don't burn

MOKA POT - I love a good cup of coffee in the morning no matter where I've laid my head. Commonly known as an espresso pot, you can put these on the fire too, just be careful of plastic handles - they melt

MORTAR AND PESTLE - good for venting . . . and for bringing out the flavour

MUSSEL MEASURING TOOL - essential if you're to play by the rules

OLIVE STONE REMOVER/GARLIC CRUSHER - a nifty two-in-one

OYSTER KNIFE - using a screwdriver should carry a health warning

PANCAKE PAN - I still use the one my grandmother taught me to make pancakes in. It's almost 29 years old - they just don't make them like they used to

POTJIE POTS - one of every size, stack them into one another so they don't take up too much space

PAELLERA - just makes paella so much easier to prepare

PASTA POT - good for blanching and steaming too

PASTA MAKER - fresh is really so much better

PEELER - sometimes skins are just too hard to eat

PIZZA SCOOP - sometimes there's a good reason to be authentic

POT HOLDER - chef's scars aren't always cool

SAUSAGE FUNNEL - to use with your mincer

SCISSORS - just one of those essentials

SIEVES - can be used for steaming. Get one or two rubber ones that will fold flat for when you travel

SMALL POTS AND PANS - that fit into one another for when you're travelling

SMALL FRUIT KNIFE - useful for what it's intended

SPATULA - cleans out bowls best

TIN MUGS - these have so many uses

TEA STRAINER - useful to use for a bouquet garni - put all your herbs inside it and chuck it in the pot with your potjie

TIN GLASSES - when you're roughing it you don't really want breakables so these are great for a Bloody Mary, G&T or even wine

TRAVELLING KNIFE - a good sharp knife that you don't mind losing

WHET STONE - for sharpening knives

WOODEN SPOONS - a winner

WHISK - get a range of sizes

WUSTHOF CARVING KNIFE - for thin slices

SKINNING KNIFE - *my pièce de résistance!*
It's made out of mild steel - which rusts like
crazy - but when you sharpen it on a whet stone
you get a mighty-fine, razor-sharp blade that's
good for everything

ALCHEMY THE BASIC BUILDING BLOCKS OF COOKING

You don't have to be a wizard in the kitchen to produce magic flavours. There just has to be the right chemistry between you and your ingredients, and you must be prepared to try anything once.

A good place to start is to take one of each of the fresh veggies in your fridge and pantry or garden and chop them into similar size chunks. Try a piece of each raw and if it's really good, that's it: no cooking needed. Then roast them in a well-oiled pan in an oven at 180°C. After 10 minutes cut off a small piece of each and taste. Remove those that are done. Keep doing this every 5 minutes or so until they're all out - simple really. Now there'll be some that just didn't cut it. They might be cooked but they just didn't look or taste right - too hard, too soft, too shrivelled or too stringy. So try something different like boiling, blanching, steaming or frying. Never cook for longer than necessary, so you need to keep testing.

Now introduce some catalysts - herbs, spices and other condiments. Start mixing and matching - meat and fish, raw and cooked, thick and thin, crisp and moist, sweet and sour. Don't be afraid to chop and change, add and subtract until the combinations are to your taste.

Baking is more of a precise science and I suggest that you start with pancakes, like I did, and then progress to breads and muffins and finally to tarts and cakes. Follow the recipe to the letter until you've grasped the concept, and then, when you're feeling confident, start with minor adjustments.

The challenge is to please all the senses: when your eyes see wow, your nose smells hmmm, your taste buds say this melts in the mouth, and your ears hear the flavours exploding on the tongue, then you'll know that you've created pure gold. And that feels great. Pure alchemy.

It's time for us all to get our hands dirty and there's nothing quite as gratifying as being able to say 'everything in this dish comes from my garden'. We don't all have large tracts of land on which to grow copious produce but you'd be surprised how much a door-sized space can yield, as long as you have prepared the soil properly before planting.
Of course you can also grow most things in pots if you don't have space for a garden bed.

STARTING YOUR OWN VEGETABLE GARDEN

Vegetables grow best where they get morning sun and if you can stick your veggie patch close to your kitchen door and a water source this will make things a whole lot easier. Also make sure that you can reach all the plants from pathways so you don't need to trample all over the bed when harvesting.

Soil needs air, water and nutrients for seeds to germinate and for small plants to grow bigger and produce healthy fruit, so slap in plenty of organic matter. If you don't already have a compost heap get started on one right away. In the mean time to prepare your veggie bed you'll need about one black bag of cardboard and paper and about two of organic waste - this can be fruit and vegetable peels, pot scrapings, egg shells, bones, lawn cuttings, dry leaves, manure, seaweed, in fact anything that will rot.

Now dig out the topsoil about one spade-head deep, and pile it on one side. Dig out the next layer of subsoil, also about a spade-head deep and put on the other side. Get rid of large stones and pieces of glass, tin etc. Loosen the soil at the bottom of the trench with a fork then cover with a layer of cardboard. Chuck in a layer of the organic waste and then cover with subsoil and water well. Carry on with these layers and watering until the trench is nearly full. End with the topsoil that you've mixed with a generous amount of rich well-decomposed compost - if your own isn't ready yet get some from your local nursery. Work this in and level the bed using a rake or a flat piece of wood. On top of this spread a layer of mulch - dry grass, straw or leaves will do fine. Don't worry if the bed is over full because it'll sink slowly as the rubbish decomposes.

Now you can start to plant. Get down and dirty - use your hands for this *(wear gloves if you like)*. Part the mulch and make a furrow in the soil. Carefully sow the seeds in the furrow, not too thickly, but always a few more than you'll need in case some don't come up. If too many germinate give them to a friend or neighbour - get everybody gardening. Cover the seeds with soil and press them down well, then water gently using a watering can with a rose attachment on its spout.

In hot, dry weather cover the seeds with a very thin layer of mulch but move this away as soon as the seedlings break through the earth. Check the soil once or twice a day to make sure that the seeds don't dry out.

Depending on the size of your family, you could have a constant supply of fresh veggies and herbs all year round. Just plant smart. Remember to plant only what you'll eat, and sow seeds at intervals during their planting season so they don't all bear at the same time. Follow the instructions on the packets. Start with tomatoes, carrots, green peppers, radishes, leeks, spinach, kale, lettuce, parsley, rocket and anything else that suits your lifestyle.

Tips // ① Make sure that your seeds are fresh. ② As a general rule, seeds should be sown at a depth of three times their own size. ③ With very fine seed, like carrots and lettuce, mix a teaspoon of seed with a cup of fine, dry sand before sowing.

WORM FARM

We live in a consumer-driven society that has the habit of using up the natural resources and not giving anything back. Can we fix what they've broken? The permaculture movement thinks so - simply by integrating our human environment with natural cycles.

One easy way of doing this is to use organic waste like peels and pips, dead flowers and leaves to start a worm farm. This gets an organic loop going. Worms eat waste and turn it into vermicompost which you dig back into the soil and then grow healthy food and flowers, and so on.

Worms are one of the major players in the decomposition of organic matter. A worm farm is practically odour and fly free *(see below how to avoid fruit flies breeding)* and compact enough to keep on your balcony, in the kitchen or even in your bedroom, and what it produces is agricultural gold that will recondition the soil for generations to come.

HOW TO CREATE YOUR OWN FARM

If money is no object, buy a ready-made worm farm. Check the web to find a supplier near you. If not, make your own, which is much more fun anyway.
① You need to score three wooden or plastic containers that fit on to one another - they can be bins, buckets or crates - and one lid.
② Drill about 50 very small holes in the bottom of two of the containers. Place a piece of cardboard snugly in the bottom of one and put some shredded newspaper soaked in water on top as bedding for your worms.

③ Now you're ready for some composters. Worms thrive in a rich, heavily mulched environment where moisture and food is supplied. Most popular are red wigglers and red earthworms. You can get them from local produce markets and certain nurseries.
④ Place the worms on the bedding and cover with shredded kitchen waste and some sheets of wet newspaper, and then place this container on top of the one with no holes. Put the third container on top and close with the lid. The worms will eat their way to the top of the middle container and when this one is

filled with 'processed' food they will start moving up into the crate above into which you must now put the food. The middle container is now full of compost so empty it out into your garden and place it on top.
⑤ In the bottom container you'll be gathering the liquid fertiliser which drips through. Use this on your pot plants and watch them turn into superplants.
⑥ Keep feeding and repeating this cycle and in no time whatsoever you'll see the benefit in your garden and know that you've started giving back and become part of the solution.

Tips on how to handle the fruit flies // ① *Always bury food waste under damp sheets of newspaper as these will act as a barrier to smells that attract fruit flies.* ② *Make a trap by putting a little vinegar, wine or fruit juice into a jar covered with cling wrap into which you have pricked a few small holes. The flies will go in through the holes and get stuck.* ③ *Kill the eggs or larvae by first freezing, boiling or microwaving the fruit and vegetable skins before placing them in the worm bin.*

A green salad should be as cool and crisp as a sparkling meadow with droplets of sun-kissed oil and tangy vinaigrette shimmering on its leaves. Here are some tips on how to pep up your rabbit food without turning it into bunny chow.

GREEN SALADS

Look around the markets which offer a wide variety of either loose or mesclun packets of pre-selected leaves. Of course you could always go one better and grow your own. Whichever way you choose, as a general guide try to include slightly bitter chicories, like endive and radicchio, peppery rocket, baby spinach and slightly sweet anise-flavoured fennel leaves. Then for variations in texture and colour maybe add some frisée or curly red leaf lettuce. **Plan on about 2 cups of mixed greens per person.**

The beauty of a mesclun mix is that it's pre-washed. Washing and, particularly, drying the leaves properly is a pain in the butt. But it's very necessary so that they're not limp and the water on them doesn't dilute the dressing. A salad spinner is a handy kitchen gadget and actually works. These are available everywhere. Better still, you might pick one up for next to nothing at a local car boot sale. Otherwise, after shaking off most of the water, rolling the leaves in paper towel helps absorb the moisture.

OTHER INGREDIENTS

Once you have your leaves you can go wild and add any number of things. Personally, I prefer to go for one or two cracker ingredients - but to each his own.

Good old standbys include: **tomatoes** - any kind will do but baby rosas would be my choice and they're readily available; **onions** - the red ones are sweeter and not quite as strong; and then there are **cucumbers, shredded carrots, shredded cabbage, avocados, olives, celery, radishes, bean sprouts** . . .

Lightly steamed or blanched and chilled veggies also make excellent salad additions: **asparagus, green beans, sugar snaps, mangetout, broccoli, cauliflower, peas, baby corn** . . .

Fruit can add unexpected flavours and colour: **small amounts of fresh berries like mulberries, cape gooseberries, strawberries, blueberries or raspberries. Orange or grapefruit slices and fresh pineapple go really well with dark greens like spinach. Add a tropical feel with fruits like mango or papaya or fresh pomegranate seeds.**

Roast vegetables on the grill or in the oven for a slightly charred flavour: **onions, zucchinis and firm mushrooms like portobellos.** Add them warm or cold.

Some more potent flavours can be added in small quantities for a big effect: **crumbled bacon bits, hard boiled egg, strong cheeses like gorgonzola, roquefort or feta, brine-cured olives like kalamatas, toasted nuts and seeds or anchovies.**

For a change, instead of toasting nuts, try them sugared. **To make your own** take about 2¼ cups of pecans or walnuts and combine with 1 cup sugar and ½ cup of water in a heavy skillet. Cook the mixture over a medium heat until the water evaporates and the nuts have a crystal, sugary appearance. Pour the nuts onto a baking sheet covered with waxed paper and immediately separate with a fork. Allow to cool before adding to salad. Store any left over nuts in an airtight container.

To make a complete meal out of any salad just add grilled or smoked chicken or beef, biltong or tofu.

DRESSING THE SALAD There is nothing that says 'global warming' louder than a wilted iceberg lettuce floating aimlessly in a sea of dressing. Salads need only about 1 teaspoon of dressing per serving and should always be tossed lightly.

A light vinaigrette dressing allows the flavours of the salad to come through. Basic vinaigrette is about 1 teaspoon vinegar to 3 teaspoons oil. Always sprinkle the vinegar first and toss, then sprinkle the oil and toss again. If you do it the other way around, the oil will prevent the vinegar from attaching to the leaves. Season with salt and pepper.

Experiment with the huge selection of oils and vinegars now available. Try red or white wine vinegars, balsamic or seasoned rice vinegar.

Just don't overdo it as the taste can easily overpower all other flavours. Substitute an acidic fruit juice for all or part of the vinegar - try lemon, lime, orange, apple or pineapple juices.

Extra virgin olive oil is always a good bet but you can play with the flavour by adding part walnut, hazelnut or almond oil. A few drops of sesame oil will give your salad an exotic Asian flair.

For another dimension to your dressings, try adding ingredients like minced shallot, garlic, ginger, onion or green onion or a small amount of mustard, horseradish, honey or soy sauce to the dressing. A sprinkle of chopped fresh herbs will take it to another level - try basil, thyme, chives or tarragon. Experiment and have fun!

A FEW COMBINATIONS TO TRY

Mixed green salad with warm goat's cheese is very trendy and so easy to make at home. Simply take a log of goat's cheese and cut it into slices about 5 cm thick. Lightly coat the cheese slices with either seasoned breadcrumbs or finely chopped nuts. Arrange on a lightly greased baking sheet and place under the grill. Grill until the cheese just starts to melt. Watch it carefully because it takes less than a minute and if you leave it too long you will end up with a runny mess! Remove from the oven and use a wide spatula to transfer the cheese slices on to a serving plate of dressed, mixed greens.

Here are some other favourites, but you really should mix and match and make them your own.

① **baby spinach, strawberries, toasted pecans and crumbled blue cheese in a balsamic vinaigrette**

② **any mixed leaves, thinly sliced red onions and mandarin orange segments sprinkled with orange juice vinaigrette and toasted pine nuts**

③ **rocket, chopped tomato, thinly sliced onion, avocado and bacon bits. Serve with a creamy blue cheese dressing**

④ **chopped fennel and red leaf lettuce with sliced mango in rice vinegar vinaigrette with a touch of sesame oil. Top with toasted sesame seeds**

⑤ **packet of mesclun, shredded carrot, shredded red cabbage, crumbled bacon bits, crumbled feta and sugared walnuts**

THANK
YOU

The debts of gratitude incurred in the creation of this book are many, but fewer, however, than the number of friends that made it possible in the first place.

My thanks must start with my mom Jeanne, without whom, literally and figuratively, none of this would've been possible. Thanks, Bean.

And then, in no particular order, other than that's how they've popped into my mind, my family and friends: my wife Eugenie, my dad Carlos, my sister Bliss, my son Dan, Richard Mills, Dale Rodkin, Fran Zwiers, Wes Volschenk *(aka Skunky)*, Evan Haussmann *(Eve-Ready)*, Duane Howard, James *(Mom)* Bell, Richard *(Porker)* and Ali Walker, Vik *(Vickie Vale)* Norval, Danny van der Merwe, Bo and Cas van den Zanden, Quint *(Squint)* Bruton, Roshni and Erik Haraldsen, Taz Wilde, Sunel *(Sunella)* Haasbroek, Danny *(Danny K)* Kodesh, Gareth *(Fish Fingers)* and Lisa Beaumont, Eben Smal, Simon Malherbe, Andrew Rawbone-Viljoen, Robbie Fivaz, Jason Abrahamse, Penny Naude, Mireille *(Miggy)* McGregor, Jenny Reay, Gordon Nasser, John Sebastian Esongo, Neil Simpson, Graham *(Brooky)* and Sandy Brookman, Lize and Stewart, Paidric O'Meara, Tamsin Reilly, Nerine Pienaar, Terry Hoffman, John Bull Harrison, Xoliswa Patricia Matana, Garth *(Mort)* Morton, Wilding Penderis, Inka Kendzia, Sean Ou Tim, Melissa Thorne, Darren *(Dad)* Putter, Andy Lupp, Andrew Faber, Evan Maclachlan, Gordon Mcallister, James Warne, Ludgero, Debi Shabason, Kate Kvalsvig, Marlese Lenhoff, Peter Adolphs, Corné Van Rooyen, David Weiland *(who had the faith in my humble idea right at the beginning)* and Keith Floyd *(the first, the one and only)*.

On a serious note: the real rock stars of Penguin who encouraged us to play - more specifically, Louise Grantham, Claire Heckrath, Renée Naudé and Pam Thornley, and to David Schröder, who contacted us with the idea for the book in the first place.

Quint *(funny how one whiskey started our friendship)* and Toby from **twoshoes**, the best creative team on the planet!

Duane Howard and Evan Haussmann for their mind-blowing photographs.

And last, but not least, Mart Raubenheimer *(Smart)*, my co-writer. Thank you, you rock, brother.

In the words of Ford Fairlane, rock 'n roll detective, you're all un$#&%#@* believable.

Justin
PS: If your name should be here and it's not - OOPS.

INDEX

Once Cooked,

Always Cooked

Yes yes, I know it's wrong to have taken the key, but it's really pretty.

Come to the Cooked side!!! We have truly FUNNN!!! there are some moments in my life... Most of them were with Cooked.